STRIKE HAPPY

A Farcical Comedy in Three Acts

by

DUNCAN GREENWOOD

SAMUEL  FRENCH

LONDON

NEW YORK TORONTO SYDNEY HOLLYWOOD

ESSEX COUNTY LIBRARY

STRIKE HAPPY

Presented by the Court Players at the Prince's Theatre, Bradford, on 29th June 1959 with the following cast of characters:

(in order of their appearance)

CLARA HELLEWELL	*Sylvia Melville*
ELSIE HELLEWELL, Clara's daughter	*Norma Graham*
ALBERT HELLEWELL, Clara's husband	*George Malpas*
GEORGE SEEGAR, Elsie's fiancé	*Alan Helm*
BENJAMIN TAPEWORTH, a Civil Servant	*Martin Carroll*
MRS FLANNEL, an ex-variety actress	*Jill Hixon*
ROSIE FLANNEL, Mrs Flannel's daughter	*Mary McKinley*
YVONNE	*Reta Franklin*
ESTELLE	

The play produced by DOEL LUSCOMBE

The action of the play passes in the living-room of Albert Hellewell's house in the industrial North

ACT I

SCENE 1   Early morning in spring
SCENE 2   Later that evening

ACT II

The following evening

ACT III

Early the following morning

Time—the present

STRIKE HAPPY

ACT I

SCENE I

SCENE—*The living-room of Albert Hellewell's house in the industrial North. It is early morning on a bright spring day.*

The room is clean and neat; the furniture old-fashioned, but serviceable. On the R of the room is a window which looks out on to a yard. In front of the window is a table and three chairs. Below the window there is an arm-chair, and above the window a door which leads to the scullery. Backstage C is a large Welsh dresser with plate-racks above, and cupboards below. Backstage up L is a recess, forming a small lobby in which there is a hat-stand. A door from the lobby leads directly to the street. There is a third door L, leading to a small passage which gives access to the rest of the house. Downstage L is an old-fashioned fireplace, armchairs are placed above and below it.

When the CURTAIN rises, the room is empty. The table is set for breakfast. Elsie's stockings are hanging on a line from the fireplace. CLARA HELLE-WELL enters R from the scullery. She carries a pot of tea and a plate of toast. She places the tea and the toast on the table, crosses to the lobby and picks up some letters and the morning paper from the mat. She moves to the door L and calls.

CLARA. Elsie!
ELSIE (*off*) Yes?
CLARA. It's on the table.
ELSIE (*off*) All right, Mum, I shan't be a minute.
CLARA. Is your dad out of bed yet?
ELSIE (*off*) I don't think so.
CLARA. Well, before you come down just nip into his room and turn his bedclothes back. He may be on strike but it's not a stay-in one. (*She crosses to the dresser, glancing at the letters as she moves. She puts the paper on the R end of the dresser and goes to the table. She sits in the chair above the table, pours herself a cup of tea, and butters a piece of toast. She opens one of the letters and starts to read it*)

(*ELSIE enters through the door L. She moves down to the fireplace, takes her stockings off the line, sits in the armchair above the fireplace and starts to put them on*)

ELSIE. Any letters for me?
CLARA. No, were you expecting one?

ELSIE. Well, not really.

CLARA. Then you won't be disappointed, will you?

ELSIE. No, but I was half expecting an explanation.

CLARA (*looking up from her letter*) Explanation?

ELSIE. And an apology for what happened last night.

CLARA. Who from? George?

ELSIE. Yes.

CLARA. What's he been up to?

ELSIE. Nothing, really.

CLARA. He's not been taking any liberties I hope. You want to put your foot down if he has, Elsie, I stood no nonsense from your father, even after we were engaged.

ELSIE. It's nothing like that, George isn't that type.

CLARA. All men are that type. Some are just slower than others, that's all.

ELSIE. If that was the only problem I'd got to face I'd know how to deal with it.

CLARA. I'm glad to hear it, but right now your immediate problem is catching that eight-thirty bus. So I'd get your breakfast if I were you.

ELSIE. I don't want any.

CLARA. Now, for Gawd's sake, Elsie, don't tell me he's putting you off your food. I could understand it if you'd only just met him. But not after you've been engaged to him for eighteen months.

ELSIE (*almost in tears*) Well, as things are at the moment I won't be engaged to him much longer.

CLARA (*rising and going to Elsie; surprised*) Elsie love, Elsie, whatever's the matter.

ELSIE. Nothing.

CLARA (*sitting on the arm of the chair; comforting her*) I think you'd better tell your old mum all about it and we'll see what we can do to make things right.

ELSIE. You can't do anything. No-one can.

CLARA. Now that's just where you're wrong. You'd be surprised what your old mum can do when she sets her mind to it. There's nothing much I don't know about the ways of men. I haven't steered your father through the seas of matrimony for twenty-five years for nothing. So come on now, tell me what it's all about.

ELSIE. Well, it's silly, really, you'll probably laugh when I tell you.

CLARA. I'll do nothing of the sort.

ELSIE. Well, it's just that George seems to take me for granted. He scarcely notices me sometimes. In fact, I might be just part of the furniture—if you know what I mean.

CLARA (*grimly*) I know what you mean all right. Though I must say it seems a bit premature to me.

ELSIE. Premature?

CLARA. Those symptoms aren't usually noticeable until you've been married at least six months. I think you're right to be worried, love. It sounds a bit serious to me.

Elsie (*bursting into tears*) Oh, Mum!

Clara (*hastily*) Not that there's nothing you can do about it, far from it, if you still love him.

Elsie. Oh, I do.

Clara. And he still loves you. You're sure about that, I suppose?

Elsie (*uncertainly*) Yes—yes, I think so.

Clara. You don't sound very sure.

Elsie. How can I be? When he spends more time at those stupid political meetings than he does with me. That's what happened last night. We were going to the pictures and he called it off at the last minute because he'd got to attend some silly strike committee meeting.

Clara (*crossing back to the table*) Well, now you've put your finger right on it. You have indeed. There's your trouble. Other interests. It's a disease they all catch sooner or later. It used to be greyhounds with your father until I put a stop to it.

Elsie. How did you do that?

Clara. Started backing horses with the housekeeping money.

Elsie. Oh, Mum, you didn't!

Clara. I did. After a few weeks on bread and marge, he came to heel all right. You can always get at 'em through their stomachs. Now he daren't put a bob each way on the Derby without asking my permission first.

Elsie. That's all very well, but I don't see how I could get at George through his stomach.

Clara (*pouring a cup of tea*) You don't have to. Get at him through his politics. Join the Conservative Party.

Elsie. That wouldn't do any good. George can always get the better of me in an argument, especially on politics.

Clara. Oh, I can see you've got a lot to learn, Elsie. If you're thinking of entering into matrimony as badly equipped as that, it'll be a failure, right from the start. (*Picking up the cup of tea and crossing to Elsie*) There, if you're not going to have anything to eat you'd better drink this.

Elsie (*taking the cup from her*) Thanks.

Clara. Unless you're prepared to argue and stand up to your husband . . .

Elsie. I don't want to argue with George.

Clara (*astounded*) You don't want to?

Elsie. No.

Clara. Then how do you propose to train him?

Elsie. George'll do what I want because he loves me. I won't force him to do anything. I'll get him to do what I want by appealing to his better nature.

Clara. Oh, I wouldn't rely on that too much if I were you, love. It's far better to assume he hasn't got any. You do know where you stand then. *(She crosses to the dresser, picks up a tray and goes behind the table)* However, if you don't feel inclined to cross swords with him, why not take a leaf out of his own book and do the same as him.

ELSIE. What do you mean? Join the Strike Committee?

CLARA. No. Go on strike yourself. *(She begins to stack the dishes on the tray)*

ELSIE. But I can't. The office staff isn't involved in this dispute.

CLARA. No, I mean go on strike with him. Break off your engagement. Refuse to see him again till he comes to his senses.

ELSIE. Do you think it would work?

CLARA. 'Course it would. If you're sure of him. Anyway, that's what I'm going to do with your father.

ELSIE. With dad?

CLARA. Yes. He's been on strike now for a fortnight, living like a gentleman and thoroughly enjoying himself. What's wrong with me doing the same? I can tell you, Elsie, we've a lot to put up with, we have. Men! Just look at 'em. They come out without so much as a mention of it to us womenfolk who've got to carry on just as before, whether we like it or not. And we're expected to make ends meet on their strike pay, which hardly pays the rent. And what for, I ask you? To establish the right of going to the lavatory without having to ask the foreman first.

ELSIE. It's not quite as simple as that, George did explain it to me.

CLARA. Oh, yes, I've no doubt he did.

ELSIE. He said they were striking to establish the inherent right of every man to stand up against oppression and tyranny.

CLARA. Well, I've never heard it put quite like that before, but I've no doubt it boils down to the same thing in the long run. And as far as your father's concerned, I'm going to establish my rights. The right to a say in things which directly concern me, and the right to take what action I think fit if that's denied me.

ELSIE. What are you going to do?

CLARA. Well, for one thing I'm going to make your father look after himself—cook his own meals.

ELSIE. But dad can't do that, he's never even boiled an egg in his life.

CLARA. Then he'll have to learn, won't he?

ELSIE. To be quite honest, Mum, I don't think I could stand by and watch dad struggling with a frying-pan without giving him a hand.

CLARA. You won't have to. You and I are moving out to your Auntie Dora's down the road.

ELSIE. But she hasn't got room. With George in digs there . . .

CLARA. That's all right, everything's fixed up. George is coming here and taking over your room—on a bed-sitting-room basis, I'm taking out the gas fire and putting in a gas ring. And as far as your father's concerned, he can have one of the attic bedrooms and cook on a primus.

ELSIE. Why put him in the attic? Can't he stay in his own room.

CLARA. No, I'm letting it to a Mr Tapeworth. I advertised it the other night in the *Evening Chronicle*.

ELSIE. But, Mum . . . ?

CLARA. Oh, I know we've never done it before. But I've got to find money somehow. I can't make ends meet on what your father's bringing in at the moment.

ELSIE. I can pay you more . . .

CLARA. No, you can't. You'll need every penny of your money for the wedding, and after. Anyway, it's all arranged. I've got Mr Tapeworth's reply here. (*She holds up the letter*) He's coming round this morning to look at the room. That's why I want your father out and the place cleaned up before nine o'clock, which reminds me . . . (*She crosses to the door* L, *opens it and calls*) Albert!

ALBERT (*off*) Hello?

CLARA. Are you still in bed?

ALBERT (*off*) No.

CLARA. Well, hurry up and come downstairs. I've something important to tell you.

ELSIE. Doesn't he know?

CLARA. Not yet. (*She moves to* R *of Elsie*)

ELSIE. Well, I don't think you ought to have made all these arrangements without giving him some idea of what you were up to.

CLARA. You've a lot to learn, Elsie. You have indeed. If you'd been struggling with men on the battlefield of life as long as I have, you'd realize that it's much more effective to let your guns off all at once rather than one at a time.

ELSIE. And how long do you propose to continue with these arrangements?

CLARA. Until the strike's over.

ELSIE. But this Mr Tapeworth. What if he's still here?

CLARA (*crossing to the* R *end of the dresser*) Well, of course, if he likes us and wants to stay on afterwards we can always push him in the attic and bring your father out.

(ALBERT *enters* L. *He is unshaven. He wears trousers, a waistcoat which is undone and a shirt without a collar*)

ALBERT (*moving above Elsie*) Good morning, all.

ELSIE. Good morning, Dad.

CLARA (*tight-lipped*) Good afternoon.

ALBERT (*crossing to Clara*) What do you mean "good afternoon"? It's nobbut eight-thirty.

ELSIE. Goodness! So it is. I must fly. (*She gets up, crosses to the hatstand and puts on her hat and coat*)

ALBERT. I'm sorry you're not with us, Elsie. It would have helped the cause if the office staff had come out in sympathy with us.

Elsie. There was no need. We have different arrangements. We don't have to put our hand up when we want to leave the room.

(Elsie *exits up* l *to the street*)

Albert. She's getting a bit too smart with her answers is our Elsie.

Clara. She's not the only one.

Albert. Has the paper come?

(Clara *takes the paper from the dresser and hands it to him*)

Thanks. (*He crosses to the armchair above the fireplace, settles himself down comfortably and opens the paper. With satisfaction*) Well, we don't seem to be much nearer a settlement.

Clara. So I see. (*She returns to the table and continues to stack the dishes on the tray*)

Albert. I reckon it could go on for quite a bit yet.

Clara. I shouldn't wonder.

Albert. A couple of weeks at least if not more.

Clara. I've no doubt.

Albert (*taking a sly look at her*) Ah, well, I suppose we'll just have to make the best of it. (*Sitting up*) By Gow, that's the stuff to give 'em.

Clara. What is?

Albert. Just listen to this. (*Reading from the paper*) " 'No Surrender,' says union leader. 'We fight till our rights are established. The bosses must be made to realize that they are dealing with human beings, not dogs.' " Good, eh?

Clara. I don't think so. From my experience the difference isn't all that obvious.

Albert. Now then, Clara, there's no need for levity. The working man of this country has been downtrodden far too long. The bosses must be put in their place and made to realize that as we're an essential part of the organization we've a right to a say in things which directly concern us.

Clara. Go on.

Albert (*encouraged at her apparent agreement; warming to his theme*) As I see it, labour and management are inseparable partners like—um—like——

Clara. —Man and wife?

Albert (*assenting*) Man and wife. And with all partnerships there should be no unilateral decisions taken by either side.

Clara. And if there are?

Albert. Then the other side has the right to strike.

Clara. Well, I must say that was very clearly put, Albert.

Albert (*flattered*) Oh, I have studied the problem, you know. I'm not like some of them down there who don't even know what they're striking for.

Clara. No, I will say that for you. You've certainly got brains and intelligence. And you do like to see justice done.

Albert. I do that. I . . . (*He suddenly notices she is clearing the table*) Wait a minute, love. You're a bit quick off the mark, aren't you? I haven't had my breakfast yet.

Clara (*taking the tray of crockery to the door* r) You're too late.

(Clara *exits* r)

Albert. Too late?

Clara (*off*) The strike started five minutes ago.

Albert. Don't talk daft, it's been going on for a fortnight.

(Clara *enters* r)

Clara (*moving to* c) Not this one.

Albert. What are you talking about?

Clara. My strike. The one I've just started.

Albert. Have you gone off your head or summat?

Clara. No. I'm just exercising my rights.

Albert. Your rights?

Clara. Yes. Like you said a few minutes ago. If one side takes unilateral action, the other side has the right to strike. You did say that, didn't you?

Albert. Yes, but . . .

Clara. That's what I thought. From now on you can do your own shopping, cook your own meals and make your own bed.

Albert (*rising and putting the newspaper on the armchair*) Now wait a bit, Clara. I think you're taking what I said just a bit too literally.

Clara. Am I? But I thought you mentioned husbands and wives in particular.

Albert. I did nowt o't'sort. It was you. Look, for heaven's sake don't try and twist things. If I thought for one moment that you were really serious.

Clara. I am.

Albert. Then you must be off your head and no mistake.

Clara (*going up to him*) I've never been saner in all my life. It's about time we women stuck up for ourselves. You men have had it all your own way far too long. For years now we've watched you all behaving like children. Well, even children have to grow up sometime, and as far as you're concerned that time's come. So now we know where we stand. When you go back to your work, I'll get back to mine. In the meantime you can look after yourself. And for a start you can cook your own breakfast. I'm going upstairs to make the beds.

(Clara *exits* l. Albert *stands stunned for a moment. He looks at the table, then at the dresser. He goes to the dresser, opens the cupboard, brings out some cheese on a plate, a tumbler and a bottle of beer. He cuts a huge slice of bread, puts a large lump of cheese on it, doubles the bread over and*

makes it into a sandwich. He then opens the bottle of beer and pours it into
the tumbler. Muttering to himself he starts to eat the sandwich and drink
the beer.

GEORGE *enters up* L *from the street. He carries a suitcase which he*
dumps in the lobby. He is a young man in his mid-twenties)

GEORGE. Hello, anyone at home? (*He moves below the* L *end of the*
dresser)

ALBERT. Aye, me—in here. Oh, it's you, George. (*He takes a*
drink)

GEORGE. 'Morning, Albert. What are you doing? Celebrating?

ALBERT. No. I'm having me breakfast.

GEORGE (*moving to the table and sitting in the chair left of it*) Well,
don't be too long about it. The meeting's due to start in about half
an hour's time.

ALBERT. I don't know that I'm going.

GEORGE (*surprised*) You're not?

ALBERT. No.

GEORGE. But it's important. They'll be taking a vote and we
want as much support as possible. If we don't get it we'll all find
ourselves back at work on Monday. And you wouldn't like that,
would you?

ALBERT. Who says I wouldn't.

GEORGE. You did. Yesterday morning. You told me that being
on strike was better than going for a holiday to Morecambe.

ALBERT. Blackpool.

GEORGE. Well, Blackpool then.

ALBERT. I wouldn't be seen dead in Morecambe.

GEORGE. Look, it doesn't matter whether it was Morecambe,
Blackpool or Southport; the point is, you liked the idea of being on
strike yesterday, and today, for some reason, you don't. Why?

ALBERT. Well, I've been thinking.

GEORGE. Go on.

ALBERT. And I've come to the conclusion that idleness is good
for no man. When you've nothing to do you get lazy and careless.
That's what's happening to me. So the sooner I get back to me bench
the better.

GEORGE. I don't believe you.

ALBERT. I don't care whether you do or you don't.

GEORGE. Who's been getting at you?

ALBERT. No-one. As a matter of fact I've always thought we
came out for a daft sort of reason. I've never had to go to the foreman
yet to ask if I could . . .

GEORGE. But for heaven's sake, Albert, surely you've realized
that it's the principle that matters in this case. We're fighting to
establish a right. And if this right's denied us, others will be, too—
more important ones. Where would we be today if everyone in the
past had behaved like you?

ALBERT. Well, I know where I'd be. I'd be here. With three square meals a day and a comfortable bed to lie on.

GEORGE. No, you wouldn't. You'd be a slave. We'd all be slaves. At the mercy of our employers, working long hours under dangerous conditions. And our womenfolk'd still be toiling down the mines pushing coal trucks.

ALBERT. Well, I don't know as I should object to that.

GEORGE (*astonished*) You wouldn't?

ALBERT. No. Not as far as Clara's concerned. She's pretty handy at pushing folk around, so I reckon she'd be able to manage a coal truck or two.

GEORGE. Oh, I see. So that's it. You've had a row.

ALBERT. We've had more than a row. She's gone on strike as well.

GEORGE. Gone on strike?

ALBERT. Aye, she refuses to make any more meals for me until I go back to me work.

(GEORGE *starts to laugh*)

Nay, it's nowt to laugh at. It's a serious business I can tell you. I'm not much of a cook and I certainly don't relish the prospect of living on bread and cheese for the next few weeks.

GEORGE. Look, if that's all that's worrying you—forget it. Leave it to me. I'll cook your meals for you.

ALBERT. Nay, I wouldn't ask you to come over here from your digs every time I wanted something to eat, George.

GEORGE. You won't have to. I'll be here—on the spot. Hey, wait a minute, hasn't she told you?

ALBERT. Told me what?

GEORGE. That I'm moving in here.

ALBERT. To stay?

GEORGE. That's right. I'm your new lodger. From today.

ALBERT. Well, I'll go to me Aunt Fanny's.

(CLARA *enters* L *carrying a pile of soiled sheets*)

CLARA. You haven't got one. 'Morning, George. (*She crosses in front of Albert to George*)

GEORGE. 'Morning, Mrs Hellewell.

ALBERT (*coming down to* L *of Clara*) Now look, Clara, George has just been telling me . . .

CLARA. That he's coming here to stay?

ALBERT. That's right.

CLARA. And so he is. I think you'll find your room quite satisfactory, George. I've put a gas ring up there so you'll be able to do your own cooking. If you fry any fish, open all the windows, and if you come in late at night borrow Albert's key. The rent's two pounds ten a week which is what you've been paying at my sister's, and if it's not asking too much I'd be obliged to receive your first week's rent in advance.

GEORGE (*rising*) That's all right. Here you are. (*He takes two pounds ten shillings from his wallet and hands it to Clara*)

(*CLARA drops the sheets on the floor in front of her and takes the money*)

CLARA. Thanks very much. That's two quid for the kitty—(*she puts two pounds in her apron pocket*) and ten bob's for you. (*She hands a ten-shilling note to Albert*)

ALBERT. For me?

CLARA. Your allowance for the week.

ALBERT. Me allowance?

CLARA. To buy your food with.

ALBERT. Ten bob? For food?

CLARA. It should be enough.

ALBERT. What do you think I am? A ruddy canary?

CLARA. That's quite enough of that, Albert Hellewell. (*Picking up the sheets*) If you can't manage you know what to do. Go out and earn some more. (*To George*) And now, George, if you're ready you can take your baggage to your bedroom.

GEORGE (*moving between Clara and Albert to the lobby and picking up his suitcase*) Right. Which one is it?

(GEORGE *moves to the door* L)

CLARA. First on the left at the top of the stairs.

ALBERT. Hey, wait a bit. That's our Elsie's room.

CLARA. I'm well aware of that.

ALBERT. Nay, hang it all, I'm fairly broad-minded, but if you're putting them in together, I think they should at least get wed first.

CLARA. Albert Hellewell, are you suggesting that I would condone immorality?

ALBERT. I don't know about condoning it, but if they share a room, I don't see how you could stop it.

CLARA (*moving to the door* R) They're not sharing a room. George'll be there on his own.

ALBERT. And what about Elsie?

CLARA. She's moving out—with me—to Dora's.

(CLARA *exits* R, *slamming the door behind her*)

ALBERT (*moving to the scullery door; stunned*) Well, I've never heard anything so daft in all me life. The next thing she'll be turning the place into a blooming dosshouse.

(*There is a knock on the door up* L)

(*Turning*) Come in.

(MR TAPEWORTH *enters carrying a brief-case and an umbrella. He is a precise middle-aged Civil Servant. He wears a dark suit, bowler hat and horn-rimmed spectacles*)

TAPEWORTH (*moving below the* L *end of the dresser*) Good morning.

ALBERT. 'Morning. Gas Company?

TAPEWORTH. Pardon?

ALBERT (*crossing to Tapeworth*) Have you come to read the meter?

TAPEWORTH. Oh, no. I've come to take up my accommodation as we agreed.

ALBERT (*astonished*) To what?

TAPEWORTH. To take up the accommodation you advertised.

ALBERT (*to George*) Blimey, what did I tell you?

(GEORGE *puts his suitcase down*)

TAPEWORTH. I trust there is no mistake. You are Mr Hellewell, I hope?

ALBERT. I am.

TAPEWORTH (*turning to George*) And this is your son?

ALBERT. No—George Seegar—your fellow lodger.

TAPEWORTH. Oh, I see. How do you do?

GEORGE (*crossing to Tapeworth and shaking his hand*) How do you do?

TAPEWORTH (*to Albert*) My name is Tapeworth. Benjamin Tapeworth. (*Eyeing George*) Your good lady will no doubt have told you of my requirements.

ALBERT. Your what?

TAPEWORTH. My requirements. The necessity of having a room to myself and remaining undisturbed during certain times of the day. You see I have important reports to prepare and a communal existence would not be conducive to intense concentration which I find absolutely necessary if I'm to carry out the function I'm paid to perform.

ALBERT. Well, that's very interesting. If you hang on a minute. I'll get an interpreter. (*He crosses to the scullery* R *and calls*) Clara!

CLARA (*off*) Hello.

ALBERT. There's a fellow here to see you—a Mr Tapeworm.

TAPEWORTH. Not "worm", Mr Hellewell.

ALBERT (*calling out*) A Mr Knotworm.

TAPEWORTH. No, no, no. The name is "Tapeworth".

ALBERT. Well, why didn't you say so in the first place.

(CLARA *enters* R *and crosses to Tapeworth* C)

CLARA. Ah. Good morning, Mr Tapeworth.

TAPEWORTH. Good morning.

CLARA. I see you've met my husband and Mr Seegar.

TAPEWORTH. I have indeed. And I feel sure we shall all get along splendidly together. A little bachelor coterie, as you might say.

ALBERT (*moving to* R *of Clara*) A what?

CLARA. Don't show your ignorance.

ALBERT. Nay, I was nobbut asking . . .

CLARA. Well, don't.

(*There is an awkward silence for a moment*)

GEORGE (*backing towards the door* L) I—um—I think I'll just nip up to my room and get rid of my bag.

CLARA. You know your way, George.

GEORGE. First on the left up the stairs.

CLARA. That's right.

GEORGE. See you later.

(GEORGE *exits* L)

CLARA. I expect you'd like to have a look at your room as well, Mr Tapeworth.

TAPEWORTH. If it doesn't inconvenience you, Mrs Hellewell. I'll just get my bags from the car. (*He turns to go and suddenly remembers something*) Oh, there is one thing . . .

CLARA. Yes?

TAPEWORTH. I feel somewhat dusty and dishevelled after my journey. Would it be in order if I were to ask for a bath?

CLARA (*surprised*) Now?

TAPEWORTH. If possible.

CLARA (*doubtfully*) Well, I'm not sure whether the water's very hot at the moment.

ALBERT. Not that it'd make any difference if it was because we haven't got a bath to put it in.

TAPEWORTH (*a little astonished*) I beg your pardon?

CLARA (*giving Albert a black look*) My husband means that we haven't yet got a bathroom.

TAPEWORTH (*apprehensively*) No bathroom?

CLARA. I'm afraid not. The plans are in for one. In fact, the landlord was only saying last week that we shouldn't have long to wait now.

ALBERT. That's nowt to go by. When them tiles came off the roof he promised to do summat about it right away. But we had a bucket int'attic catching the drips for eighteen months.

CLARA. Take no notice of him, Mr Tapeworth, he always looks on the black side of things. If you want a bath you shall have one.

ALBERT. Even though it'll only amount to a sponge down in front o't'fire.

TAPEWORTH. A sponge down?

ALBERT. In a hip bath.

TAPEWORTH. Oh dear!

ALBERT. Nay, it's not so bad. You get used to it. When you've been doing it as long as I have you won't even notice the neighbours popping in and out.

TAPEWORTH (*aghast*) The neighbours . . . ?

CLARA. Albert! That's enough. There's nothing to worry about, Mr Tapeworth. The doors are always locked on bath nights.

TAPEWORTH. I'm glad to hear it.

CLARA. And, of course, Albert'll fill the bath for you.

ALBERT. He'll what?

CLARA (*ignoring him*) And you can have this room to yourself, and when you've finished Albert'll empty the bath.

ALBERT. He'll do what . . . ?

CLARA (*cutting in*) So I don't think you'll find it too bad.

TAPEWORTH (*uncertainly*) No—no, perhaps not.

ALBERT. Of course, I suppose you realize that a bathroom isn't the only thing we haven't got.

TAPEWORTH. No? Oh, dear, you don't mean . . . ?

ALBERT. That's right, through the scullery and down the yard.

CLARA. Albert!

ALBERT. So now that you understand the position I've no doubt you'll be wanting to look round for somewhere else.

TAPEWORTH (*after a slight hesitation*) No—no, I never go back on my word. I think the inconveniences—(*he laughs nervously*) if I may call them that . . .

CLARA. You may.

TAPEWORTH. Are sufficiently small not to warrant any change of plans on my part.

CLARA. Well, now, I'm right glad to hear you say that, Mr Tapeworth, I am indeed. (*With a look at Albert*) There aren't many people nowadays who are willing to face up to their obligations and responsibilities.

TAPEWORTH. That's very true, Mrs Hellewell.

CLARA (*edging Tapeworth to the door up* L) So now, if you like to get your suitcases I'll show you up to your bedroom. I don't think you'll be disappointed. It's the best room we've got. On the first floor at the front of the house.

TAPEWORTH. Good. I shan't be a moment.

(TAPEWORTH *exits up* L *to the street*)

ALBERT (*crossing to Clara*) Hey, wait a bit, Clara, that's our bedroom.

CLARA (*crossing below him to the dresser*) It was.

ALBERT. 'Ow do you mean—it was?

CLARA (*turning at the dresser*) I'll be sleeping at Dora's from now on. (*She opens the cupboard in the dresser*)

ALBERT. Now, look here, Clara, there's a limit to everything. I don't mind making my own meals, and I'll put up with you and Elsie clearing off to your sister's, but if you think for one moment that I'm going to share my bed with—that! (*He nods his head towards the door up* L)

CLARA. I don't. You'll be sleeping in the attic. I've moved your things up there already. (*She takes out a frying-pan and a primus stove from the cupboard*)

ALBERT (*in horror*) The attic? (*He moves to Clara in front of the dresser*)

CLARA. That's right. (*She puts the frying-pan and the primus stove into his hands*) And you can take these with you when you go up. You'll need them.

(ALBERT *puts the frying-pan and the primus stove on the dresser, crosses to the lobby, takes his cap, muffler and jacket from the hatstand and puts them on.* CLARA *watches him curiously*)

CLARA. And where do you think you're going?
ALBERT. To the strike meeting—to register me vote.

(GEORGE *enters* L)

GEORGE. Hello, have you decided to go after all?
ALBERT. I have. Are you ready?
GEORGE. Sure.
ALBERT (*crossing to the scullery door*) Come on then, we'll go out the back way. (*He opens the scullery door*)

(GEORGE *goes through into the scullery*)

(*He locks the door behind George and takes out the key*) I suppose the back door's locked?
CLARA. Yes.
ALBERT. Good. Here's the scullery key. (*He puts it on the table*) Don't let him out for an hour. The less opposition I have the better.

ALBERT *crosses to the lobby and exits up* L *to the street as—*

the CURTAIN *falls*

SCENE 2

SCENE—*The same. Later that evening.*

When the CURTAIN *rises,* CLARA *is discovered above the table, setting it for one. There is a vase of flowers on the dresser.* ALBERT *is hanging about near the door of the scullery. He suddenly picks up some plates from the dresser, crosses to the table and places them on it.* CLARA *looks at him curiously. He smiles at her, returns to the dresser, picks up a cruet, and returns to the table. He places it on the table and smiles at her again.*

CLARA. What's the idea?
ALBERT. Eh?
CLARA. I said what's the idea—making yourself useful all of a sudden?
ALBERT. I was only trying to be helpful.
CLARA. It's a pity you didn't start trying twenty-five years ago.
ALBERT. I . . . (*He is just about to argue with her, but thinks better of it*) You've forgotten the butter. (*He smiles again, crosses to the dresser,*

picks up the butter dish, and returns to the table) There, I think that's about everything. Except the flowers. (*He crosses again to the dresser, picks up a vase of flowers and returns to the table with it*) It's a long time since we've had flowers in the house.

CLARA. It's a long time since you've brought any home.

ALBERT. Well, I've made up for it today.

CLARA. So I see.

ALBERT. You know I just said to myself coming home, if there's one thing Clara likes it's a bunch of flowers.

CLARA. Did you now?

ALBERT. I did.

CLARA. Which way did you come home? Through the cemetery?

ALBERT. No, I didn't. Those flowers were bought with five shillings of that ten bob you gave me.

CLARA. And I suppose the rest's gone on beer?

ALBERT. It has not. I've got it here in me pocket.

CLARA. Well, hang on to it, you'll need it.

ALBERT. Nay, I don't know as I shall, now that you're coming round a bit. (*He crosses to the armchair above the fireplace*)

CLARA. What do you mean—now that I'm coming round?

ALBERT (*turning*) Well, making me tea for me. By Gow, it smells good. What is it? Bacon and egg?

CLARA. And chips.

ALBERT (*sitting in the armchair*) I'll enjoy that. You know bread and cheese is all very well, but there's nothing like a good square meal when you're really feeling hungry.

CLARA. Then you'd better go upstairs and cook yourself one.

ALBERT (*crestfallen*) Cook myself one?

CLARA. That's what I said.

ALBERT. That's what I thought you said.

CLARA. That bacon and egg in there is for Mr Tapeworth.

ALBERT (*dejected*) Oh.

CLARA. Any further comments to offer?

ALBERT. No—except . . .

CLARA. Except what?

ALBERT. Couldn't you just shove another egg in the pan? It wouldn't take up much room.

CLARA. I'm afraid not. You know very well what my terms are. You get back to your work and I'll get back to mine.

ALBERT (*rising*) Nay, dammit all, Clara, I'm trying as hard as I can. Why do you think I locked George up this morning? (*He crosses to L of the table*)

CLARA. It didn't do much good, did it?

ALBERT. Can I help it if I was outvoted? I did me best. When they asked for a show of hands for a return to work, I put both mine up. I can't do more than that. I think you're being most unreasonable. Particularly after I've been thinking of you all day, wondering how I can help you, buying you flowers—and . . .

CLARA. It's no good, Albert, you can't get round me like that.
So you'd better face up to it. You've wasted your time.

(CLARA *exits to the scullery* R)

ALBERT. I've wasted more than me time, I've wasted ~~five bloom-~~
ing bob!

(GEORGE *enters from the street carrying an evening paper. He takes off
his cap and hangs it on the stand. He eyes Albert coldly*)

'Evening, George.
GEORGE. 'Evening.

(*There is a pause.* GEORGE *crosses to the armchair above the fireplace
and sits*)

ALBERT (*taking a pace towards George; making conversation*) It's a bit
cooler, isn't it?
GEORGE. Much.

(*There is a pause.* GEORGE *starts to read the evening paper*)

ALBERT (*taking another pace towards George*) Have you had any-
thing to eat?
GEORGE. Yes.
ALBERT. You're lucky.
GEORGE. Eh?
ALBERT. I said you're lucky.
GEORGE. Why?
ALBERT. Because I haven't. (*He pauses*) Er—I'm sorry about this
morning, George. (*He moves to* R *of George*)
GEORGE. So you said before.
ALBERT. It's not that I'm against the strike, it's just that, well,
I'm in a difficult position. For one thing I'm getting a bit fed up of
bread and cheese.
GEORGE (*suddenly bursting out*) And for another, you're just a
selfish old man who thinks of nothing but his own personal comfort,
and if it wasn't for the fact that Elsie takes after her mother, I'd
think twice of taking you on as a father-in-law.
ALBERT (*after a pause; very quietly*) I'm sorry you feel like that,
George. I was only doing what I thought was best.
GEORGE. For yourself.
ALBERT. Aye, I suppose so. But it hasn't made much difference.
The strike's still on. (*Moving up stage. Dejectedly*) Ah well, I suppose
I'd better go upstairs and try and light me primus. (*He turns, hesitating
a moment*) I don't suppose you happen to have a box of matches on you?

(GEORGE *takes a box from his pocket and tosses it across to him*)

(*Catching the box*) Thanks. I've never actually lit one of them things
before, but I don't expect it's very difficult. (*He pauses*) I fancy you
just pump it a bit and then put a match to it.

(GEORGE *ignores him*)

Don't you?

GEORGE. Uh? (*Looking up from his paper*) Yes, something like that.

ALBERT. That's what I thought. (*He moves to the door* L)

(CLARA *enters from the scullery* R, *carrying a plate of bacon, egg and chips. She puts the plate on the table.* ALBERT *eyes it hungrily. She gives him a look.*

    CLARA *exits* R.

    ALBERT *crosses to the table a nd picks up a chip from the plate*)

CLARA (*off*) Albert!

ALBERT (*arrested in the act of putting the chip into his mouth*) Yes, love?

CLARA (*off*) Leave those chips alone.

ALBERT (*hastily replacing the chip*) I've not touched them, love.

CLARA (*off*) Well, I'll know if you have. I've counted them.

(ALBERT *moves dejectedly away from the table to* C)

GEORGE. Why don't you go out for a meal?

ALBERT. I can't. I've nobbut five bob left to last for the rest of the week.

GEORGE (*grinning*) All right. Give me the matches back.

ALBERT (*taking the box out of his pocket; brightening up*) You mean you'll light me primus for me?

GEORGE. I'll do more than that. I'll cook you a meal. When old Tapeworm's finished his.

ALBERT (*going up to him and giving back the matches*) George. That's real decent of you. Ee! By Gow, I've always said our Elsie was lucky in finding a fellow like you.

GEORGE. That's all very well. But there's one condition attached to all this.

ALBERT. Aye? What's that?

GEORGE. From now on you fight—on both fronts. Agreed?

ALBERT. Agreed.

(*They shake hands.*

    MR TAPEWORTH *enters* L *and crosses to* C, *in front of the dresser. He carries his brief-case*)

TAPEWORTH. Oh, good evening, gentlemen. I was right, I see.

ALBERT. What about?

TAPEWORTH. The smell.

ALBERT. What smell?

TAPEWORTH. The delicious aroma invading the establishment. I judged from it that my evening repast was ready. And I must say I am ready for it.

(CLARA *enters from the scullery* R, *carrying a teapot which she places on the table*)

CLARA. Oh, there you are, Mr Tapeworth, I was just going to get Albert to call you. It's all ready. (*She pulls out the chair above the table*)

TAPEWORTH. So I see. Am I to dine alone? (*He moves to the table and sits in the chair*)

CLARA. Yes, if you don't mind.

TAPEWORTH. Not at all. I was just wondering about my other two companions here . . .

ALBERT. Well, if you really want someone to keep you company, Mr Tapeworth. (*He makes a move towards the table*)

CLARA. That won't be necessary. Mr Tapeworth is quite happy to eat on his own, aren't you, Mr Tapeworth?

TAPEWORTH. Oh, yes, indeed.

CLARA. Well, now, I think you'll find everything there on the table. If you do happen to want something else Albert'll get it for you.

TAPEWORTH. Thank you very much. (*He starts his meal*)

CLARA. Not at all. Now if you'll excuse me I'll get on my way. (*She crosses to the lobby and puts on her hat and coat*) I'll be back in the morning to see to your breakfast. Good night.

TAPEWORTH⎱
GEORGE ⎰ (*together*) Good night.

(CLARA *exits up* L *to the street*)

TAPEWORTH. Your good lady explained to me in her letter that she was staying at her sister's.

ALBERT. That's right. For a while anyway. It's a matter of accommodation. (*He crosses to* L *of Tapeworth and watches him hungrily*)

TAPEWORTH. Quite. As far as I'm concerned it's an admirable arrangement. The presence of women can be so very distracting. Do you not agree, Mr Seegar?

GEORGE. Eh? Oh, yes—yes.

TAPEWORTH. At the last place I stayed, the daughter of the house spent most of her time encouraging me to learn how to perform a rather barbaric dance which I believe is popular at the present time. However, I wasn't a very apt pupil.

GEORGE. You didn't get very far with it?

TAPEWORTH. No, she gave up teaching me after a time. It appears I'm a square.

ALBERT. A what?

TAPEWORTH. A square, Mr Hellewell. A technical term for a beginner I understand.

ALBERT. Oh, I see.

TAPEWORTH. I was glad that her interest in me had evaporated, somewhat. But then her mother took over and I was obliged to listen to long and gruesome accounts of her numerous operations. It's amazing how many removable organs women seem to possess. As a result of all that I scarcely got any work done.

GEORGE. I take it you're not married, Mr Tapeworth?

TAPEWORTH. Good gracious me, no. I live with mother.

GEORGE. And she doesn't disturb your work?

TAPEWORTH. On the contrary. I find her most helpful. I discuss my work with her and she gives me advice on all my problems. If it hadn't been for her I should probably now be bound by the chains of matrimony. There are so many designing females about these days, Mr Seegar, ready to pounce on an eligible young bachelor like myself, that is a comfort to know that I have always someone to fall back on for advice and protection.

ALBERT. That's right, Mr Tapeworth. You can't be too careful. You stay single as long as you can.

TAPEWORTH. Oh, I intend to. My work keeps me far too busy to allow me any time for dalliance.

GEORGE. What is your line of business?

TAPEWORTH. I am a Civil Servant.

ALBERT. Then I wasn't far wrong when I mistook you for a gas meter inspector.

TAPEWORTH (*coolly*) My job carries a little more responsibility than that. I've been sent here to mediate in a most frivolous and ridiculous strike which is going on in this town.

GEORGE (*putting the newspaper down; suddenly interested*) Really?

TAPEWORTH. Yes. You would hardly believe it if I told you that grown men were actually striking in a factory not far from here for a most childish and unnecessary reason.

ALBERT. I wouldn't at all. As a matter of fact . . .

GEORGE (*rising and cutting in*) We've both heard about it and we entirely agree with you.

ALBERT (*taking a step towards George*) What do you mean we entirely agree with him? Why, it's nobbut five minutes ago since you said . . .

GEORGE (*moving to R of Albert; cutting in*) That the strike weapon should never be used frivolously.

ALBERT (*gazing at George in astonishment*) Eh?

TAPEWORTH. Quite right, Mr Seegar. It's gratifying to know that there are people with sensible ideas like yourself.

ALBERT. Now wait a bit, George, let's just get this clear. I've been under the impression all along that you . . .

GEORGE. Were against the strike? (*He makes signs at Albert, unseen by Tapeworth, indicating that he wants him to keep his mouth shut*)

ALBERT. Aye—no!

GEORGE. Well, you're quite right. I am.

ALBERT. What?

GEORGE. Against it.

(ALBERT *suddenly realizes George is playing some deep game.* GEORGE *moves to the R end of the dresser*)

ALBERT. Oh, I see, well, of course, that's what I meant in the first place.

TAPEWORTH. So we are all agreed. I trust, however, that you will treat what I have told you as confidential. The opinions I have expressed are my own. As a Government servant I must be impartial. And my final report will be based on an unbiased assessment after hearing both sides. And now, if you'll excuse me, I'll repair to the sanctuary of my room to prepare my plan of campaign for tomorrow. Your wife, Mr Hellewell, is an excellent cook. That meal was delicious. (*He rises, picks up his brief-case and goes to the door* L. *He turns to face them*) Good night to you both.

(TAPEWORTH *exits* L)

ALBERT (*moving to* L *of George*) And now perhaps you'll explain what the devil that was all about.

GEORGE. Sh! (*He crosses below Albert to the door* L, *opens it, looks out and shuts it again*)

ALBERT. Well? (*Moving to* C)

GEORGE. What a streak of luck!

ALBERT. What is?

GEORGE. That fellow coming here. (*Going to Albert*)

ALBERT. Why?

GEORGE. Oh, use your loaf. He's come to investigate the strike, hasn't he?

ALBERT. Aye.

GEORGE. And he's going to take evidence from both sides and then report. Right?

ALBERT. Right.

GEORGE. So if he reports in our favour.

ALBERT. Which he won't.

GEORGE. Why not?

ALBERT. Well, you heard what he said.

GEORGE. He'll change his tune when we get to work on him. We'll influence him and make sure his report is made in our favour.

ALBERT. How?

GEORGE. You wait and see. I've got some ideas but I'll need your support.

ALBERT. My support?

GEORGE. Yes. Play up to him. Gain his confidence. Don't antagonize him. Fill his bath up for him . . .

ALBERT. Now wait a bit, George. There's a limit to everything.

GEORGE. Oh, for heaven's sake, Albert, show a bit of sense, you want the strike over, don't you?

ALBERT. I don't know.

GEORGE. What do you mean—you don't know?

ALBERT. Well, one minute you're all for it and the next minute you're all against it. So how the heck do you expect me to know what I want.

GEORGE. Look. If the strike's over by the week-end and we've won our case, everyone'll be happy, won't they?

ALBERT. Aye.

GEORGE. Well, that's what we're after, and that's what'll happen if we play our cards right.

ALBERT. Are you sure?

GEORGE. 'Course I'm sure.

ALBERT. Then I'm for it—I mean agin it—I mean whatever you say.

GEORGE. Good. Now this calls for a celebration, where's the beer? (*He moves up to the dresser, opens the cupboard door and brings out three bottles and two tumblers*) Ah, here we are.

ALBERT (*following George to the dresser on his left*) Hey, now steady on, George. I've got tomorrow's breakfast to think of.

GEORGE (*opening two of the bottles*) You can get some more.

ALBERT. I've told you. I've nobbut five bob to last me till the end of the week.

GEORGE. Don't worry. The strike'll be over by then.

ALBERT. I hope you're right.

(TAPEWORTH *enters* L)

TAPEWORTH. Excuse me. I just came back to see whether all would be clear for my ablutions this evening.

ALBERT (*turning*) Your what?

TAPEWORTH. My bath.

ALBERT (*looking at* GEORGE, *who nods*) Oh, er, yes—yes, that'll be all right, Mr Tapeworth. When do you want it?

TAPEWORTH. Well, if it's at all convenient, almost immediately. I could then nip into bed and study my papers in comfort.

ALBERT. I'll see to it at once.

TAPEWORTH. Thank you. Thank you very much indeed.

ALBERT. Would you like a clean towel?

TAPEWORTH. If there's one available I'd be most obliged.

ALBERT. Leave it to me.

(TAPEWORTH *exits* L)

(*To George*) How am I doing?

GEORGE. Fine. (*He hands Albert a glass of beer*) Here's something to keep your strength up.

ALBERT. Thanks.

GEORGE. To success! (*He drinks*)

ALBERT. To success. (*He drinks*) And may we never have another ruddy strike as long as I live. (*He drinks again*)

(ELSIE *enters up* L *from the street. She moves towards the door* L)

GEORGE. Elsie!

ALBERT. Hello, love, this is a surprise.

ELSIE (*coldly*) Hello, Dad. 'Evening, George.

ALBERT. What's happened? Have you decided to change your mind?

ELSIE. No. I've decided to change my dress. I'm going to the pictures.

GEORGE (*drinking up his beer*) Give me five minutes and I'll join you.

ELSIE (*coldly*) Why? Haven't you got a meeting to attend.

GEORGE (*putting his glass down on the dresser*) I don't go to meetings every night.

ELSIE. No? (*Coming down to* R *of the armchair above the fireplace*)

GEORGE. No.

ELSIE. Where do you go then?

GEORGE. Well, I take you to the pictures sometimes.

ELSIE. That's right, sometimes. But not tonight.

ALBERT. Now I don't want to butt in . . .

ELSIE (*cutting in*) Well, don't.

ALBERT. I was only going to say . . .

ELSIE (*cutting in*) I'm not interested.

ALBERT. Well, if that's how you feel . . .

ELSIE (*cutting in*) It is.

ALBERT. In that case, I'll go and get old Tapeworm's bath ready.

(ALBERT *exits to the scullery* R)

GEORGE (*taking a step towards Elsie*) Now perhaps you'll explain what all this is about?

ELSIE. I thought I had explained. It's quite simple. I'm going to the pictures—without you.

GEORGE. Why?

ELSIE. Because I've arranged to go with someone else.

GEORGE. Who?

ELSIE. Ernest Parsons.

GEORGE. That drip!

ELSIE. He's not a drip. He's something you'll never be.

GEORGE. What?

ELSIE. A gentleman.

GEORGE. Pshaw! Just 'cos he wears a bow tie and talks as though he'd got a plum in his throat.

ELSIE. Not at all. I think he's a gentleman because he's unselfish, considerate and attentive.

GEORGE. And I'm not?

ELSIE. Quite.

GEORGE. Well, I've never heard of anything so stupid in all my life. You can't go out with him.

ELSIE. Why not?

GEORGE. Because you're engaged to me.

ELSIE. I was.

GEORGE. What do you mean you was.

ELSIE. Were.

GEORGE. Were then.

ELSIE. I mean it's all over, George. We're through. And to prove it you can have your ring back as well. (*She pulls off her engagement ring and throws it at George*)

(ALBERT *enters from the scullery* R, *carrying an old-fashioned hip bath. The ring misses George and lands in the hip bath*)

ALBERT. Hey, what's the idea? Chucking things at folk.
ELSIE. I'm sorry, it was meant for George.
ALBERT. Well, make sure you hit the right target next time.
ELSIE. I will.
ALBERT (*crossing to the fireplace with the bath and placing it on the hearthrug*) I don't want to be in the way when you start on the ornaments.
ELSIE. I've said I'm sorry.
ALBERT (*grumbling*) It might have put my eye out.
ELSIE. Oh, for heaven's sake stop going on about it.
ALBERT. All right—all right. Keep your hair on. (*He picks the ring out of the bath and offers it to her*) You'd better have it back.
ELSIE. It's not mine.

(ALBERT *offers it to George*)

GEORGE. It's not mine, either.
ALBERT. Well, for heaven's sake make your minds up who it does belong to. I can't very well leave it in the bath.
GEORGE. Why not?
ALBERT. Old Tapeworm might sit on it.
GEORGE. Let him.
ALBERT. Nay, we can't have him walking about with a diamond-studded tiara. His mother might object.
GEORGE. Let her.
ALBERT. Well, if that's how you feel, I'd better look after it myself till you come to your senses. (*He crosses back to the scullery door* R) And when you want it back, give me due warning. It might not be readily available.

(ALBERT *exits* R)

GEORGE. Well?
ELSIE. Well what?
GEORGE. I'm waiting.
ELSIE. For what?
GEORGE. An explanation.
ELSIE. I should have thought the position was quite clear. Our engagement's off, and I'm going out with someone else. And now, if you'll excuse me, I'll go and change my dress.

(ELSIE *exits* L)

GEORGE (*following her to the door* L) Elsie, Elsie. Come back here . . .

(ALBERT *enters from the scullery* R *with a bucket of water*)

Of all the stupid senseless creatures! (*To Albert*) Do you know what she's gone and done? She's broken off our engagement.

ALBERT. You don't say. (*He crosses to the bath and pours the water into it*)

GEORGE. And what's more she's going to the pictures with Ernest Parsons. (*He moves to* R *of the armchair above the fireplace*)

ALBERT. Ernest Parsons?

GEORGE. That fellow with a beard who works in the drawing office.

ALBERT. Oh, him. Well, I wouldn't let it worry you.

GEORGE. Wouldn't let it worry me! My God! It's all very well for you to talk. You don't know what it's like to be thrown overboard.

ALBERT (*cutting in*) 'Course I do. Her mother did the same to me three times. And come to think of it, one of the chaps she chucked me for had a beard. A big curly black one. He was a sailor.

GEORGE. I'm not interested in what Clara did to you.

ALBERT. Well, you ought to be. It's nobbut ten minutes since you were congratulating yourself on the fact that Elsie took after her mother. So you can't very well complain when you suddenly find out that she does.

GEORGE. Are you suggesting that she's likely to break off our engagement at least three times.

ALBERT. Nay. I wouldn't go as far as to say that. After all she's my daughter as well, you know. So she's not completely irresponsible.

GEORGE. I should hope not.

ALBERT. In fact, I wouldn't mind betting that her mother's behind all this.

GEORGE. You mean she's deliberately persuaded Elsie to break off our engagement?

ALBERT. Aye—as part of her end-the-strike campaign. Don't you see? They're both trying to make things as difficult for us as they can so we'll chuck in our cards. When the strike's over, she'll come crawling back, you'll see.

GEORGE. Do you really think so?

ALBERT. 'Course I do. Anyway, you needn't let the grass grow under your feet in the meantime. Do what you've told me to do. Fight back.

GEORGE. How?

ALBERT. Take someone else out and let her know about it. Make things as difficult for her as she's making them for you. For a start you could go upstairs and chuck her out of your bedroom. I've no doubt that's where she's doing her changing act.

GEORGE. That's a damn good idea. (*He goes towards the door* L)

(TAPEWORTH *enters through the door* L *and almost collides with George.* TAPEWORTH *carries his brief-case, a sponge bag, and a small attaché-case. He is in his dressing-gown*)

TAPEWORTH. Excuse me.
GEORGE. Excuse *me*.

(GEORGE *exits* L)

TAPEWORTH. Ah, Mr Hellewell. I hope I'm not intruding. I just popped down to see if the jolly old tub was ready to receive me.
ALBERT. By the look of you I thought you were going on your holidays.
TAPEWORTH. Pardon?
ALBERT. Nothing. Just a joke. Your bath's not quite ready yet.
TAPEWORTH. Is that it? (*He points to the bath*)
ALBERT. It will be when I've filled it up. (*He crosses to the door* R)
TAPEWORTH (*doubtfully*) I see. Well, in that case I'll commence my preliminaries. (*He crosses to the table, places his brief-case on the chair above it and his attaché-case and sponge bag on the table. He opens the attaché-case*)
ALBERT (*moving to* C) Your what?
TAPEWORTH. My ante-nocturnal preparations.
ALBERT (*looking at him blankly*) Eh?
TAPEWORTH. The things I've got to do before I go to bed.
ALBERT. Oh, I see. (*Moving to the scullery door* R) Well, help yourself when you're ready. It's through the back door and across the yard . . .
TAPEWORTH. No, no, I mean I have my gargling and what not to do. It will take me at least five minutes.
ALBERT (*blankly*) Oh. Well, your bath should be ready by then.

(ALBERT *exits to the scullery* R. TAPEWORTH *takes out a throat spray, a number of bottles, a tumbler and a thermometer from the attaché-case and places them on the table. He is just about to use the throat spray when there is a loud banging off* L. *He goes to the door* L *and opens it.*

ALBERT *re-enters from the scullery* R *with another bucket of water*)

TAPEWORTH. Did you hear that, Mr Hellewell?
ALBERT. What?

(*The knocking is heard again*)

TAPEWORTH. There it is again. It must be Mr Seegar.
ALBERT (*crossing to the bath*) Eh? Oh, aye, that's right, it is. He's trying to open his wardrobe door. It sticks.
TAPEWORTH. Oh, I see. (*He shuts the door and returns to the table*)

(ALBERT *tips the bucket of water into the bath.* TAPEWORTH *uses the throat spray, then takes a pill from each of the four bottles and swallows three of them, one after another. He makes a gulping noise as each pill goes down*)

ALBERT (*watching Tapeworth; curious*) Got a 'eadache?
TAPEWORTH. A headache?
ALBERT. Aye—taking all them aspirins.

TAPEWORTH. These aren't aspirins, Mr Hellewell. They're vitamin tablets. Most essential for the efficient functioning of the body. Try some.

ALBERT. No, thanks. I don't think there's 'owt better than Epsom's myself. (*He crosses to the scullery door* R)

(*The knocking is heard again*)

TAPEWORTH. Dear me! Mr Seegar's certainly having a time with that wardrobe. Do you think he needs any assistance?

ALBERT. No. She'll open up in a bit.

TAPEWORTH. Pardon?

ALBERT (*hastily*) The wardrobe, I mean.

TAPEWORTH. Oh. I see.

(ALBERT *exits* R. TAPEWORTH *swallows the fourth pill. He takes a bottle of bath salts from his case, crosses to the bath and empties some into it.*

ALBERT *re-enters* R, *carrying a glass of water. He crosses to Tapeworth and holds it out to him*)

TAPEWORTH. For me?

ALBERT. To wash them pills down.

TAPEWORTH. A kindly thought, Mr Hellewell. But unfortunately unnecessary. They're down. (*He returns to the table, takes the thermometer and, humming to himself, dips it in the bath*)

(ALBERT *watches him, fascinated*)

(*Looking at the thermometer and smiling at Albert*) A little too hot.

ALBERT. Eh?

TAPEWORTH. The bath.

ALBERT. Oh. (*He tips the glass of water into it*)

TAPEWORTH. Hardly enough, I should think.

(ALBERT *exits* R. TAPEWORTH *moves to the table, takes his own glass and pours some liquid from a bottle of mouthwash into it. He takes a mouthful and gargles. Then he suddenly realizes that there is nowhere to spit. He looks round desperately, crosses to the fireplace and lifts the lid off the coal-box, wondering whether he dare use it. He hears Albert returning and changes his mind.*

ALBERT *re-enters* R *with another bucket of water.* TAPEWORTH *makes unintelligible signs and noises at him.*

ALBERT, *misunderstanding what Tapeworth is trying to tell him, hustles him to the scullery door.*

TAPEWORTH *is pushed off* R)

ALBERT. Straight through the back door—across the yard—mind the bucket . . .

(*A loud crash off*)

TAPEWORTH (*off*) Ugh?

ALBERT. It doesn't matter. Carry on. (*He crosses to the fireplace and tips the water into the bath. To himself*) I don't wonder he feels bad taking pills like that. It's enough to turn the strongest stomach.

(Elsie *and* George *enter* L, *arguing.* Elsie *has changed her dress*)

Elsie. It was my room until this morning.

(Elsie *and* George *move into the lobby*)

George. Well, it isn't any more, so you can clear all your stuff out of that wardrobe and do your changing at your Aunt Dora's in future.

Elsie. Don't worry, I will. Good-bye!

(Elsie *exits up* L *to the street, slamming the door after her*)

Albert. Sounds as though you're doing all right.

George (*moving to* R *of the armchair above the fireplace*) Not as well as I might have done. I didn't move fast enough. She'd locked the door and got herself changed before I could do anything about it.

Albert. You've got her rattled, anyway. What you want to do now is to follow it up.

George. Follow it up?

Albert. Aye, get after her. Sit behind her in the pictures. If nowt else occurs to you, you can at least make things uncomfortable for Ernest Parsons.

George. How?

Albert. By shoving your foot up the gap in his seat.

George. Albert, you're a genius! (*He goes into the lobby and puts on his cap. A sudden thought strikes him*) Oh!

Albert. What's up?

George. I've just remembered. I promised to cook a meal for you.

Albert. Never mind that. You can make up for it later.

(Tapeworth *enters* R)

George. I will. Cheerio!

Albert. Cheerio, and good luck.

(George *exits up* L)

Albert (*to Tapeworth*) Feeling better?

Tapeworth (*moving to* C) Oh, yes, thank you, Mr Hellewell. A most embarrassing moment. But fortunately not quite as embarrassing as the time when I lost my teeth in the tube.

Albert. Your what?

Tapeworth. My teeth. I sneezed and they landed in a lady's shopping basket. I had a terrible time trying to extract them without her noticing.

Albert. But you got them back all right?

Tapeworth. Oh, yes. But not before she'd accused me of trying to pinch her oranges.

ALBERT (*teasing him*) And didn't you?

TAPEWORTH (*taking him seriously*) Good gracious me, no. I wouldn't have dreamed of pinching anything that belonged to her. In any case, she hadn't very much to pinch.

ALBERT (*enjoying this*) You don't say!

TAPEWORTH (*quite serious*) No, her basket was almost empty. And now if you've finished filling my bath.

ALBERT. It's all ready.

TAPEWORTH. Good. I'll just nip upstairs and get my night-shirt.

(TAPEWORTH *exits* L. ALBERT *picks up the bucket and crosses to the scullery door* R.

There is a knock at the street door up L. ALBERT *puts down the bucket, crosses to the door and opens it.*

MRS FLANNEL *and* ROSIE, *her daughter, are standing outside.* MRS FLANNEL *is a florid, well made-up, middle-aged woman of about fifty. Her daughter is about twenty-three and is attractive although there is something rather cheap and flashy about her. They are carrying suitcases*)

MRS FLANNEL. Mr Hellewell?

ALBERT. That's right. Won't you come in?

(ROSIE *and* MRS FLANNEL *enter*)

MRS FLANNEL. I'm Mrs Flannel and this is my daughter Rosie.

ALBERT. How do you do?

ROSIE. How do you do.

MRS FLANNEL. We've come in answer to that advert of yours in the *Evening Chronicle*.

ALBERT (*blankly*) Advert?

MRS FLANNEL. Yes, about the room. The one you've got to let.

ALBERT (*slowly*) Oh, that—well, you see I'm afraid . . .

MRS FLANNEL. Now don't tell us it's already gone or we'll be most disappointed. Won't we, Rosie?

ROSIE. Oh, yes—ever so.

ALBERT. Well, as a matter of fact . . .

MRS FLANNEL. We're both of us most particular. We'd be no bother to you. No bother at all, I can assure you. We're scrupulously clean . . .

ALBERT. Oh, I can see that . . .

MRS FLANNEL. And we keep reasonable hours . . .

ALBERT. I've no doubt you do, but . . .

MRS FLANNEL. And we'd be prepared to pay you three pounds a week, which is a bit more than you're asking.

ALBERT (*suddenly interested*) Three pounds a week?

MRS FLANNEL. In advance, provided of course there are adequate cooking facilities available.

ALBERT (*clearing his throat*) Well—er—it isn't very much of a room. It's in the attic, but I think you'd be quite comfortable in it.

Mrs Flannel. And the cooking facilities?

Albert. There's none up there, I'm afraid, but you could use the scullery.

Mrs Flannel (*indicating the door* R) Through here?

Albert. That's right.

Mrs Flannel. Then we'll inspect that first. Come along, Rosie.

(Mrs Flannel *and* Rosie *exit* R. Albert *is about to follow.*

Tapeworth *enters* L. Albert *hastily closes the door to the scullery and stands with his back to it*)

Tapeworth. A terrible thing has happened, Mr Hellewell. Mother has forgotten to put in my nightshirt. (*He moves to* R *of the armchair above the fireplace*)

Albert. You don't say.

Tapeworth. I do.

Albert. Then you'll have to sleep in the buff.

Tapeworth. In the where?

Albert. Wi' nowt on.

Tapeworth. Oh, I couldn't do that. I should probably catch a chill. I'm most susceptible to temperature fluctuations. I don't suppose you have a spare nightshirt you could lend me?

Albert. I never wear them.

Tapeworth. You mean—you sleep in the rough, or whatever you call it.

Albert. No, I wear pyjamas.

Tapeworth. I could make do with pyjamas for once, that is, if you have a spare pair.

Albert. I dare say I could find some old ones. They may be a bit patched.

Tapeworth. That won't matter in the least.

Albert (*anxiously listening at the door to see if Mrs Flannel and Rosie are coming*) Well, if you'd like to nip up to your bedroom I'll get them for you. You can see if they fit then before you get into your bath . . .

Tapeworth. I don't think I should delay my ablutions any longer. The water's getting colder every moment.

Albert. I'll put some more hot in, whilst you're upstairs.

Tapeworth. I wouldn't dream of troubling you further, Mr Hellewell. Except, of course, for the towel you promised to get me.

Albert (*listening intently at the door*) Eh?

Tapeworth. The towel.

Albert. Oh, yes—the towel. (*He hesitates*)

Tapeworth. If it's not too much trouble.

Albert. No, no, it's no trouble, it's just that I—I er . . .

Tapeworth. Well, Mr Hellewell?

Albert. Nothing. (*He glances anxiously at the door* R *and crosses quickly to the door* L) I'll get it for you.

(ALBERT *exits* L. TAPEWORTH *moves to the table and takes off his dressing-gown, revealing long woollen underwear. He starts to take off his shoes.*

MRS FLANNEL *and* ROSIE *enter* R)

MRS FLANNEL. And now if you'll take us up to the . . .

MRS FLANNEL *and* ROSIE *suddenly see Tapeworth and both give a squeal of horror.* TAPEWORTH, *in great embarrassment, grabs his dressing-gown, and tries to conceal himself with it as he moves away from them. He walks backwards into the bath, loses his balance and sits in it as—*

the CURTAIN *falls*

ACT II

SCENE—*The same. The following evening.*

When the CURTAIN rises, ALBERT is sitting in the chair above the table, a napkin tucked in his chin. He is just finishing a meal that MRS FLANNEL has prepared for him. MRS FLANNEL is sitting in the chair L of the table. They each have a glass full of beer in front of them. A couple of empty beer bottles stand in the centre of the table. They are laughing heartily at some joke that has passed between them, and it is obvious that their relationship has become quite intimate in a short space of time.

MRS FLANNEL (*nudging him*) Oh, Mr Hellewell, you are a caution and no mistake.

ALBERT. Foreman, or no foreman, I wasn't going to stand for that.

MRS FLANNEL. I should think not indeed.

ALBERT (*putting down his knife and fork and wiping his mouth with his napkin*) Well, I feel better for that.

MRS FLANNEL. How about a nice piece of apple pie and custard to finish off with?

ALBERT. I couldn't eat another thing, Mrs Flannel. You've done me real proud.

MRS FLANNEL. A bit of home-made seed cake or some shortbread, then? They're both very nice, though I says it as shouldn't.

ALBERT. Nay, I'll have to undo me waistcoat as it is, and you wouldn't want me to go further than that now, would you?

MRS FLANNEL (*with a laugh*) Oh, Mr Hellewell, you do say some things. You're a proper comedian, you are.

ALBERT. Oh, I wouldn't say that. It's just that I'm feeling pleased with life at the moment. There's nothing like a full stomach for making a chap feel good. Do you know that's the first really square meal I've had for nearly two days? I'm not very good at fending for myself, I'm afraid. (*He unbuttons his waistcoat*) That's better.

MRS FLANNEL. What you want is a woman round the place, Mr Hellewell.

ALBERT (*giving her a sidelong glance*) Aye—I suppose it is.

MRS FLANNEL. Someone to cook your meals for you regularly and darn your socks and warm your slippers when you come home at night.

ALBERT. Aye, maybe so.

MRS FLANNEL. I always say there isn't a sorrier sight than a bachelor who has to do all them things for himself.

ALBERT. I'm not exactly a bachelor, Mrs Flannel.

MRS FLANNEL. Oh, I didn't think you were. You've got an air of experience and maturity about you which no bachelor possesses.

ALBERT. Have I?

MRS FLANNEL. You have indeed. And if you'll excuse me saying so, it's just those things about you that make you attractive to the opposite sex.

ALBERT. Do you really think so?

MRS FLANNEL. I most certainly do.

ALBERT (*sticking out his chest*) Well now. (*Impulsively*) Have another beer.

MRS FLANNEL. I don't mind if I do.

ALBERT (*he rises, goes to the dresser and gets another bottle out of the cupboard. He unscrews the stopper and refills her glass and his own*) I think before we get to know each other better, Mrs Flannel, I ought to explain one or two things to you. (*He sits in the chair above the table*)

MRS FLANNEL. No need, Mr Hellewell. I can put two and two together, and where they don't make four I've always my clair-voyance to fall back on. It never lets me down. You'd be surprised how quickly I can size people up.

ALBERT. Oh?

MRS FLANNEL. With you, for example, I don't need to read cards or look in tea-cups. You're pretty straightforward. Your aura's as plain as a pikestaff.

ALBERT. Eh? (*He glances at his waistcoat and hastily starts to button it up*)

MRS FLANNEL. Your psyche.

ALBERT (*blankly*) Oh, I see.

MRS FLANNEL (*gazing at him intently*) You're a married man, aren't you?

ALBERT. Well, I couldn't be much else if I'm not a bachelor, now could I?

MRS FLANNEL. Wait a minute, I see something else. Your wife has not long departed from you.

ALBERT. That's right.

MRS FLANNEL. You're a widower.

ALBERT. Well, I wasn't up to yesterday. But anything can happen in twenty-four hours, can't it?

MRS FLANNEL. You mean she's deserted you?

ALBERT. That's right.

MRS FLANNEL. Well, I'm very sorry to hear it, Mr Hellewell. Some folk don't know when they're well off. All I can say is that most women would be deeply and truly thankful to have a nice quiet respectable chap like you for a husband.

ALBERT. Well, that's very nice of you to say so, Mrs Flannel. As a matter of fact, it coincides with my sentiments exactly. Have another beer.

MRS FLANNEL. *Mr* Hellewell, you'll be having me tiddly if you're not careful.

ALBERT. Not on this stuff. (*He fills up her glass*)

MRS FLANNEL. Thanks ever so. Whoa! That's enough.

(ALBERT *fills up his glass*)

You know I always think that it's worse for a woman to desert a man than vikki verka.

ALBERT. Than what?

MRS FLANNEL. T'other way round.

ALBERT. Why?

MRS FLANNEL. Well, one expects a man to go off the rails more than a woman. Like my Joe. Not that I wasn't glad to see the back of him. He was incapable every night.

ALBERT. Incapable?

MRS FLANNEL. Drunk!

ALBERT. Oh, I see.

MRS FLANNEL. Bottle a day man at that time, Joe was. Mind you, we could afford it then. Topping the bill we were.

ALBERT. Topping the bill?

MRS FLANNEL. On the halls.

ALBERT. You mean the stage?

MRS FLANNEL. That's right. You might have heard of us. "Two in Harmony" we was called. Songs at the piano and all that.

ALBERT. Can't say I have. But then I never did go to the music-halls very often.

MRS FLANNEL. You'd have heard of us if you had. We played here in Broadmarsh many a time. At both the Palace and the Hippodrome.

ALBERT. Really? That's very interesting. I'd never have thought you were an actress.

MRS FLANNEL. Ex-actress, love. Haven't been in front of the footlights now for over six years. Things might have been different though if that lady conjuror hadn't joined the show at Sowerby Bridge.

ALBERT. Why?

MRS FLANNEL. Joe got too interested in her routine and finished up doing a vanishing trick with her. Mind you, I should have known what was going on. He was always in the wings when her act was on. Mucking about in her disappearing cabinet and holding her goldfish bowls for her. And I thought he was just trying to be helpful.

ALBERT. Your clairvoyance mustn't have been functioning very well at the time.

MRS FLANNEL. It wasn't. Though looking back I do remember getting certain premonitions of which I took no notice. I think perhaps in a way I was glad to be rid of him. Except for the act. It finished that, of course.

ALBERT. What did you do?

MRS FLANNEL. Carried on for a bit on my own, until Rosie was old enough to take over. As soon as she got established I retired. Now I travel around with her, acting as her dresser, adviser and general manager.

ALBERT. And Joe?

MRS FLANNEL. I divorced him for desertion.

ALBERT. Oh. (*After a slight pause*) Er—was it expensive?

MRS FLANNEL. What?

ALBERT. Divorcing him.

MRS FLANNEL. It certainly was.

ALBERT. How much?

MRS FLANNEL. I can't remember exactly, but I know it ran away with most of my savings at the time. Why? Are you thinking of following suit?

ALBERT. Oh, I wouldn't like to say that exactly. But you never know, do you?

MRS FLANNEL. You don't, Mr Hellewell. You don't indeed. Fate has some funny tricks up her sleeve for all of us. You may have been married to Mrs Wrong for the last umpteen years, and now, who knows, perhaps Mrs Right is just around the corner. (*She smiles at him coyly*)

ALBERT. Aye, may be so. But if divorce is as expensive as you suggest, I certainly couldn't afford it. I haven't any savings to fall back on. Though the tide should start to turn now that I've let those other rooms—thanks to you.

MRS FLANNEL. It was a pleasure to be of help, Mr Hellewell.

ALBERT. I don't suppose you know whether they're likely to pay their rent regularly?

MRS FLANNEL. Oh, I think so. Yvonne and Estelle are two very refined young ladies and absolutely steady. They've got to be, they do a high-wire act. (*She nudges him and laughs at her own joke*)

ALBERT. And what about the one I've put in George's room?

MRS FLANNEL. Bert Wheatly? Well, now, I don't know very much about him. You never can tell with comedians. They're apt to be a bit unpredictable. If only you'd had a bathroom, Captain Sparkler'd have come like a shot. I could have vouched for him all right. But as things are I couldn't have persuaded him. He won't go anywhere unless there's adequate accommodation for Sally.

ALBERT. His wife?

MRS FLANNEL. No, his sea-lion.

(GEORGE *enters up* L. *He takes off his hat and coat and hangs them up on the stand. He turns and notices Albert and Mrs Flannel for the first time. He looks at her in surprise*)

ALBERT. 'Evening, George.

GEORGE (*moving to* C) Good evening.

ALBERT. This is Mrs Flannel. I don't think you've met her before.

GEORGE (*going to her*) How do you do?

MRS FLANNEL (*holding out her hand*) I'm very pleased to know you.

(GEORGE *shakes her hand*)

I've heard a lot about you already.

GEORGE (*looking at Albert*) Nothing slanderous, I hope.

MRS FLANNEL. On the contrary. Mr Hellewell looks on you as a model lodger.

GEORGE (*grinning*) I can't be much else when I'm courting his daughter, can I?

MRS FLANNEL. Really, I didn't know that. (*To Albert*) So you've got a grown-up daughter, Mr Hellewell?

ALBERT. Aye. She'll be twenty-two next.

MRS FLANNEL. Twenty-two? Well, you certainly don't look old enough to have a daughter of that age.

ALBERT (*flattered*) Don't I?

MRS FLANNEL. You do not.

ALBERT. Well, of course, I married very young . . .

MRS FLANNEL. You must have.

ALBERT. And then again, the male members of my family never did show their age. My father lived to be over eighty and hadn't a grey hair on his head when he died.

MRS FLANNEL. Really?

ALBERT. And me grandfather before him he lived to be over ninety . . .

GEORGE (*cutting in*) If you'll excuse me I think I'll go up to my room. (*He moves towards the door* L *but stops* R *of the chair above the fire-place as Albert speaks*)

ALBERT (*rising*) Your room? (*In sudden consternation*) Oh, now wait a minute, George—I'd like to have a word with you first—(*nodding and winking at Mrs Flannel*) on family matters. (*He moves to* R *of George*)

MRS FLANNEL. Then I'll make myself scarce by starting the washing-up. (*She rises, gets a tray from the dresser and stacks the dishes on to it. She looks coyly at Albert as she picks up the tray. She goes to the door* R) When you've finished your little chat, I wouldn't object to you giving me a hand in the scullery.

ALBERT (*playing up to her*) You can have both of them, if you insist.

MRS FLANNEL (*giggling*) Oh, you are a one.

(MRS FLANNEL *exits* R)

GEORGE. What's the game?

ALBERT (*gazing off* R) Eh?

GEORGE. Playing up to a bit of old mutton like that.

ALBERT. What do you mean, old mutton?

GEORGE. She'll be fifty if she's a day.

ALBERT. Don't be so daft. She's nobbut thirty-nine.

GEORGE (*incredulously*) Thirty what?

ALBERT. Thirty-nine.

GEORGE. Who told you?

ALBERT. She did.

GEORGE. Then she's been counting backwards for the past ten years. Who is she, anyway?

ALBERT. One of the new lodgers. (*He moves to the chair* L *of the table and sits*)

GEORGE. New lodgers? (*Moving to him. Suddenly anxious*) Hey, wait a minute, you haven't got rid of old Tapeworm, have you?

ALBERT. No, he's still here, but I've let off one or two other rooms as well.

GEORGE. Which?

ALBERT. The top attic back.

GEORGE. Who to?

ALBERT. Mrs Flannel and her daughter.

GEORGE. And . . . ?

ALBERT. The top attic front to a couple of young ladies called Yvonne and Estelle.

GEORGE. I thought that was your room.

ALBERT. It was.

GEORGE. Then I suppose you'll be wanting to share mine.

ALBERT. No. I'm sleeping down here on a camp bed.

GEORGE. Well, that's a relief, anyway.

ALBERT. I couldn't very well share your bedroom.

GEORGE. Why not?

ALBERT. You're—er—sharing it already.

GEORGE. I'm what?

ALBERT. I've let half of it off to a chap called Bert Wheatly.

GEORGE. Now look here, Albert . . .

ALBERT. Don't think I'm pushing you out. You're at liberty to stay there. As long as you keep to your own half.

GEORGE. I've never heard of anything so high-handed in all me life.

ALBERT. Now, then, take it easy, George. After all there's two beds in it. And as I see it, there's no point of letting one lie idle when it can be earning fifty bob a week. You'll still be sleeping in comfort whereas I'll be sleeping down here on a camp bed.

GEORGE (*angrily*) I don't care whether you sleep in the kitchen sink. I paid two pounds ten for that room.

ALBERT. Not to me you didn't. You paid it to Clara. So if you want to argue. Argue with her.

GEORGE. I will, too. You—you capitalist.

ALBERT (*rising and crossing to the fireplace*) Now then, now then, there's no need to use dirty words. This is a question of self-preservation. I'd only got five bob left, as you know. I had to do something —or starve. Anyway, I don't know what you're kicking up such a fuss about. I thought you'd be pleased when you knew what I'd done.

GEORGE (*following him*) Pleased? When I've got to share my room with someone I don't even know.

ALBERT. Well, if it's a question of knowing your room-mate I'll get him to swap with old Tapeworm.

GEORGE. God forbid!

ALBERT. Then let's have less grumbling. And stop thinking of your own comfort. Think of the Cause for a change. If everyone had behaved like you in the past, where would we be today?

GEORGE. I don't see what filling the house up with lodgers has to do with the Cause.

ALBERT. Then you haven't much imagination. Can't you see Clara's face when she finds out that I'm financially independent.

GEORGE (*slowly*) Yes. By Jimminy, I think you're on to something.

ALBERT. 'Course I am. She'll be as mad as blazes. And when she hears that the lodgers are cooking my meals for me into the bargain she'll come running back as fast as her legs can carry her, only to discover that there's no room for her. Unless she cares to fix up a hammock in the scullery.

GEORGE. Albert. I'm proud of you. The battle's as good as won.

ALBERT (*crossing to up stage of the table and picking up his glass of beer*) Not yet, it isn't. We've got to be prepared for counter-attacks. Clara isn't one to give up easily. She'll try every trick she can think of, so we'd better watch out. By the way, how did you get on with Elsie last night?

GEORGE. Not so good. They sat on the back row.

ALBERT. Pity. She's won that round all right. Never mind, you get yourself fixed up with someone else, like I suggested, and make sure she sees you both out together.

GEORGE. That's not so easy.

ALBERT. Why?

GEORGE (*moving to L of the table*) Well, I don't know anyone else for a start.

ALBERT. Blimey! When I was your age I had half a dozen on a string at the same time.

GEORGE. I haven't the time to go playing that game.

ALBERT. It's not time you want, it's stamina.

GEORGE. Anyway, I haven't seen any girl I particularly want to go chasing after—except Elsie.

ALBERT (*a sudden thought strikes him*) Wait a bit, I don't think you'll need to go chasing anyone—now that Rosie's here.

GEORGE. Rosie?

ALBERT (*nodding his head in the direction of the scullery*) Mrs Flannel's daughter.

GEORGE. What's she like?

ALBERT. Well, in my day I'd have called her a bit of fluff. But then, I'm old-fashioned. Today she'd probably be referred to as a smashing bit of crackling.

(ROSIE *enters* L. *She is dressed in a kimono. She carries a pair of briefs and a brassiere*)

ALBERT (*to George*) See what I mean?
ROSIE (*stopping short*) Oh! Good evening.

GEORGE (*a little taken aback by her casual attire*) Er—good evening. (*He moves to the dresser*)

ALBERT (*propelling George towards Rosie*) Ah, Miss Flannel, this is George Seegar. Another member of our—er—happy little family.

ROSIE. Pleased to meet you, I'm sure.

(ROSIE *holds out her hand.* GEORGE *shakes it*)

ALBERT. I was just telling George about you and your mother and all the new guests we've got—and, er, how you seem to be settling down well.

MRS FLANNEL (*off; calling*) Mr Hellewell!

ALBERT. There's your mother. I'm supposed to be helping her with the washing-up.

MRS FLANNEL (*off*) I'll be finished if you don't come directly.

ALBERT (*calling*) I'm on me way now. (*He moves to the table and picks up the beer bottle*) With reinforcements. (*To George and Rosie*) Be good.

(ALBERT *exits* R, *winking at George as he goes.* GEORGE *and* ROSIE *are embarrassed*)

ROSIE. Funny old fellow, isn't he?

GEORGE. Eh?

ROSIE. Mr Hellewell.

GEORGE. Oh—er—yes.

ROSIE. What did you say your name was?

GEORGE. Seegar, George Seegar.

ROSIE. Mind if I call you George?

GEORGE. No—no, not a bit.

ROSIE. My name's Rosie.

GEORGE. Oh, is it. It's—er—a very nice name.

ROSIE. Get away, it isn't. It's such a lousy name I wouldn't dare use it on the stage. (*She moves to the armchair above the fireplace and sits on the arm*)

GEORGE. You're on the stage?

ROSIE. Oh, yes. I call myself "Sabrita".

GEORGE. Really?

ROSIE. Yes. Sounds much better than Rosie Flannel. More refined.

GEORGE. And—er—original.

ROSIE. Oh, yes. I always think there's something sort of foreign and mysterious about it, don't you?

GEORGE. Yes—oh, yes.

ROSIE. Mum thought so, too. In fact, it was her who suggested it. She was on the stage at one time herself, you know.

GEORGE. Was she?

ROSIE. Yes. But she's past it now, I'm afraid. She's my wardrobe mistress now. As a matter of fact, I came down to see if she'd mend these for me. (*She holds up the briefs and a brassiere*) I'm busting again

GEORGE. Eh?

ROSIE. Popping—at the seams.

GEORGE. Oh, I see. Couldn't you stitch them yourself?

ROSIE. I could, but she likes to do it. You see, it's one of her jobs to see that my costume's O.K. before I start my act.

GEORGE (*raising his eyebrows*) You mean you go on the stage in those?

ROSIE. You don't expect me to go on without them, do you?

GEORGE. I mean—just those?

ROSIE. With a few trimmings. These are the basic parts, of course.

GEORGE. Of course. What do you do—dance?

ROSIE. No, sing.

GEORGE. Couldn't you sing just as well with a bit more on than that?

ROSIE. I could, but the songs wouldn't be half as effective.

GEORGE. Why?

ROSIE. Because they're those sort of songs.

GEORGE. What sort?

ROSIE. You know.

GEORGE. No, I don't.

ROSIE. Coo, you're a bit dim, aren't you. Don't you ever go to a show?

GEORGE. No.

ROSIE. Never seen one on telly even?

GEORGE (*pompously*) No, I haven't got a telly. And if I had I wouldn't spend my time watching decadent bourgeois exhibitions.

ROSIE (*rising; indignantly*) Hey! There's nothing like that about my act. Even if I wanted to put that sort of stuff over the Watch Committee wouldn't let me.

GEORGE. That's not what I mean. You don't understand.

ROSIE (*cutting in*) No, and you don't understand either. Here, I'd better show you. Hold these. (*She throws the brassiere and briefs at him*)

(GEORGE *catches them*)

GEORGE. Hey! Wait a bit.

ROSIE. Don't look so scared. They're empty. I've got to have my hands free for a demonstration. Now then, you're in the front row of the stalls. (*She pushes him into the chair* L *of the table*)

GEORGE (*rising*) I'd rather be in the back row of the circle.

ROSIE. That's no good. You'd be too far away. (*She pushes him down again*) Now then, I come on like this—(*she strikes a pose*) and start off with a rousing little number which goes—(*she sings*)

> Rock, rock, rock abye baby,
> Rock rock, on the tree top.
> Come on down and don't say may be,
> We've gotta date at a ten cent hop.

And so on. That gets their feet tapping and puts them all in a good mood. Then I go into a sultry sort of number about yearning for someone to love me. And that's where you come in.

GEORGE (*apprehensively*) Me?

ROSIE. Yes. Someone like you. It's all part of the act. I come down into the audience and sing to the shyest and most bashful-looking chap I can find in the front row of the stalls.

GEORGE. I'm not bashful.

ROSIE. 'Course you are. You're just about crawling under your chair as it is. You'd be under the table if I gave you the full treatment.

GEORGE. And what's that?

ROSIE. Sitting on your knee—(*she sits on his knee*) like this, ruffling your hair—(*she ruffles his hair*) like that, and finishing up by covering your face with lipstick—like this. (*She kisses his cheeks and leaves large lipstick marks on them*)

(ELSIE *enters from the street*)

That really gets them that does.

ELSIE (*coldly*) So I should imagine. (*She moves to* C)

GEORGE (*rising quickly*) Elsie!

(ROSIE *slides on to the floor.* GEORGE *takes a step towards Elsie*)

ELSIE (*crossing below George to up stage of the table; tight-lipped*) Carry on, don't mind me. I've only come to make Mr Tapeworth's supper. Keep clear of the table and you won't be in the way. Try the easy chair, it's more comfortable.

(ROSIE *gets up and moves behind George to* R *of the armchair above the fireplace*)

GEORGE. Now, look here, Elsie . . . (*He points at her, then realizes he is holding the brassiere in his outstretched hand*)

ELSIE. I'm looking.

(GEORGE *hastily pockets the brassiere*)

GEORGE (*somewhat embarrassed*) I mean—what's the idea bursting in here like this?

ELSIE. It's a good job I did. Otherwise I might have regretted taking mum's advice and breaking off our engagement.

GEORGE. So it was her who put you up to it?

ELSIE. Yes, it was. She must have known all the time the sort of person you were.

ROSIE. Mr Seegar's doing nothing to be ashamed of.

ELSIE. He looks it, doesn't he? With a face like that and those things sticking out of his pocket.

ROSIE (*moving to the fireplace*) I think it would help if I explained what I am.

ELSIE (*cutting in sarcastically*) I don't really think that's necessary.

GEORGE. Don't be so damned insulting. Miss Flannel was only showing me what she does for a living—I mean . . .

ELSIE. Obviously.

GEORGE (*in resignation*) Oh, what's the use. (*Suddenly changing his tactics*) Oh, well, I suppose we'd better tell her the truth, Rosie.

ROSIE (*turning to him; not understanding him*) The truth?

GEORGE. Yes, tell her what she wants to know. (*Moving to Rosie. Dramatically*) That you and I are crazy about each other. And that we've been carrying on like this behind her back for the past three months.

ROSIE (*gaping at him*) Us?

ELSIE. I knew it.

GEORGE (*turning to Elsie*) Oh, no, you didn't. But you do now. And so will everyone else. (*To Rosie*) We're not afraid. Our love is big enough to blossom in the open. (*To Elsie*) That's why Rosie's come to live here.

ELSIE (*astounded*) To what?

GEORGE. To live here. (*To Rosie*) Isn't that so, Rosie?

ROSIE (*dazed*) Well, I do live here, but . . .

GEORGE (*to Elsie*) You see?

ROSIE. Yes, but . . .

GEORGE (*cutting in*) No buts. The truth is out now. There's no reason to be ashamed of it. In fact, we should be proud to let the whole world know how we feel about each other. (*Turning to Elsie and moving towards her*) Our love is a beautiful, savage, shameless, pulsating thing, Elsie Hellewell.

ELSIE (*backing away towards the scullery door; in horror*) Oh!

GEORGE. Something that you'll never understand.

ELSIE (*cutting in*) Keep away from me!

GEORGE. Because your precious Ernest Parsons is a bloodless worm when it comes to making love.

ELSIE (*recoiling*) Why you—you maniac.

(ALBERT *enters* R, *carrying a glass of beer in his left hand. He overhears the last remark*)

ALBERT. Who's a maniac?

ELSIE. George.

ALBERT. Why?

ELSIE. I can't tell you, it's too horrible. (*She clutches his left arm*) Oh, Dad!

ALBERT (*quickly changing his glass from his left to his right hand*) Mind me beer.

ELSIE. Thank goodness there are still some men you can trust.

ALBERT. What the heck are you talking about?

ELSIE. George. He's behaving like a beast.

ALBERT. To you?

ELSIE. No, to her.

ALBERT. Then what are you grumbling about?

ELSIE. I'm not grumbling. I'm disgusted. I walked in here five minutes ago and caught them carrying on together.

ALBERT. You did?

ELSIE. Yes.

ALBERT. Is this true, George?

GEORGE. Yes.

ALBERT. Then you want to be more careful in future and lock the door before you start.

ELSIE (*in horror*) You mean, you don't mind?

ALBERT. Why should I if Rosie doesn't. (*Crossing to the dresser and getting out another bottle of beer from the cupboard*) And I don't see why you should for that matter. After all, you're not engaged to him any longer. (*He winks at George*)

ELSIE (*astounded*) Dad! I'm surprised at you. Condoning such things. Why she's even admitted that she's living here with him.

ROSIE. I didn't say that.

ELSIE (*nearly in tears*) Yes, you did. (*To Albert*) And what's more, he's admitted that he's crazy about her. He even said that his love for her was a—a beautiful, savage, shameless . . .

GEORGE. Pulsating thing.

ELSIE. You see?

ALBERT. Well, that's pretty good going, George. I haven't got half as far as that in the scullery.

ELSIE. In the scullery?

ALBERT. With her mother.

MRS FLANNEL (*off*) Albert.

ALBERT (*shouting*) Coming, Agatha! (*To George*) We've only just got on to Christian name terms out there.

MRS FLANNEL (*off*) You'd better hurry up. You're getting all behind.

ALBERT. Aye, and from what I've seen in here, it's going to take me quite a bit to catch up.

(ALBERT *exits* R, *carrying his glass and the fresh bottle of beer*)

(*Off*) Here we are, more reinforcements.

(MRS FLANNEL *and* ALBERT *laugh off* R. ELSIE *gives a little squeal of horror*)

ELSIE (*almost in tears*) Oh! Just you wait until mum hears about this.

(ELSIE *exits up* L *to the street*)

ROSIE (*going to him*) Well! You're a deep one and no mistake. Talk about Jekyll and Hyde. I thought, at first, that butter wouldn't melt in your mouth. But after she came in—woo hoo! I can see I shall have to look after myself as long as I stay here.

GEORGE (*a little embarrassed*) That's all right. You needn't worry. My bark's worse than my bite.

ROSIE. I should just hope it is.

GEORGE. In fact, I haven't really got a bite at all. You see, I didn't mean all that stuff I just said to you.

Rosie (*in mock surprise*) You didn't?

George. No. I don't really know what came over me. I suppose I was just saying it to pay Elsie back for breaking off our engagement. I hope I haven't offended you or anything.

Rosie. Offended me! Huh! It'd take a bit more than that to offend me. In fact, I quite enjoyed it.

George. You did?

Rosie. Sure.

George (*relieved*) Here, have a cigarette. (*He offers her a cigarette*)

Rosie (*taking one*) Ta.

(George *takes one himself and lights them both*)

You know when you said your love for me was a beautiful, savage something or other you sounded just like Merlin Bronzo.

George. That's a pity 'cos that's who I got it from. I went with Elsie to see his latest film last week. (*A sudden depressing thought strikes him*) Oh! Do you think she twigged?

Rosie. I don't think so. You'd enough supporting evidence to convince her.

George. Eh?

Rosie. In your pocket.

George. Oh, yes.

Rosie. Talking of Merlin Bronzo. I think he's smashing, don't you?

George (*without enthusiasm*) He's all right.

Rosie. When I said you sounded like him, it wasn't just what you said, it was how you said it.

George. Was it?

Rosie. Yes. (*She is close to him looking at him intently*)

George (*a little uneasy*) Well, I don't suppose I look like him as well.

Rosie (*gazing at him*) Oh, I don't know. There is a resemblance. Maybe not physically. But you've got that same undercurrent of power, if you know what I mean.

George (*still uneasy*) Undercurrent of power?

Rosie. Yes. Didn't you know?

George. No. In fact, I don't really know quite what you mean.

Rosie. It's a sort of primitive magnetism. Attractive to the opposite sex. I knew you'd got it when you started going on at Elsie.

George (*casting an appealing glance for help at the scullery door*) Oh, did you?

(Mrs Flannel *and* Albert *can be heard laughing in the scullery off* R)

Sounds as though Albert's got it as well.

Rosie (*sliding her hands on to his lapels and up on to his shoulders*) I'm not interested in Albert.

GEORGE (*very embarrassed*) No, I don't suppose you are.

(*There is a scraping noise at the door up* L)

(*Breaking away from her and moving up stage to the* L *end of the dresser*) Look out. There's someone at the door. It's probably Elsie coming back with her mother.

ROSIE (*unmoved*) So what? (*Following him and attempting to put her arms round his neck*) We'll teach her another lesson.

GEORGE. Eh? (*Pushing her arms down*) No, no, that'd be overdoing it a bit. I don't believe in playing the same card twice. Look, don't you think you'd better go into the kitchen and get your mother to stitch these up for you. (*He takes the brassiere and briefs from his pocket and hands them to her*)

ROSIE (*pouting*) You're trying to get rid of me, aren't you?

GEORGE. No, no, it's just that if Elsie's got her mother with her, I'll need all my wits about me. I shan't be able to concentrate with a distraction like you around.

ROSIE (*smiling seductively*) I'm more of a distraction when I'm in costume. (*She holds up her brassiere and briefs*)

GEORGE. I've no doubt. (*He looks anxiously at the door up* L)

ROSIE. I'll put it on and show you, if you like.

(*The door knob on the door up* L *rattles violently*)

GEORGE (*looking round anxiously*) No!—I mean, later, when you've got them mended.

(ROSIE *is pushed off into the scullery by* GEORGE)

(*He straightens his jacket and tie and stands waiting, expecting Elsie and Clara to enter. He starts to rehearse what he is going to say. Clearing his throat*) Mrs Hellewell, before you say anything to me, I should like you to remember that it was Elsie who broke off our engagement, and if I choose a fresh partner it should therefore be of no consequence to either you or her. (*He nods his head in satisfaction, marches smartly to the door and flings it open*) Mrs Hellewell . . . (*He stops short*)

(TAPEWORTH *is standing on the doorstep. He is wearing his city suit and a bowler hat. He carries his brief-case and a rolled umbrella which he holds vertically in front of him. It is raining hard and he is very wet. He is also drunk. He walks slowly and precisely, but not unsteadily, to* C)

(*In astonishment*) Mr Tapeworth! (*He closes the door and comes down stage* L *of Tapeworth*)

TAPEWORTH. Ah, good evening, Mr Seegar. I had some difficulty in finding the keyhole. Was it you who let me in?

GEORGE. Yes.

TAPEWORTH. Then I must thank you for performing such a kindly act.

GEORGE. It was nothing.

TAPEWORTH. Ah, my boy, it was. Kindness is a rare commodity

these days and one must applaud it when one observes it. How different the world would be if one could only rely on the inherent goodness of humanity——

GEORGE. You're wet.

TAPEWORTH. —instead of on the caprice of ingenious inventions such as this—(*handing his umbrella to George*) which fail to function when required.

GEORGE (*taking the umbrella and hanging it on the hat-stand*) Are you all right?

TAPEWORTH. Perfectly. Are you?

GEORGE (*coming down to R of the armchair above the fireplace; surprised*) Me? Yes, why?

TAPEWORTH. You appear to have a gory visage.

GEORGE. A what?

TAPEWORTH. You've got a bloody face.

GEORGE. Now look here, Mr Tapeworth . . .

TAPEWORTH. No, no, my boy. I mean it. You look in the mirror and you'll see.

GEORGE (*moving to the fireplace and looking in the mirror above the mantelpiece; noticing the lipstick marks*) Oh, those—they're nothing—(*wiping them off with his handkerchief*) just the result of a shaving accident.

TAPEWORTH. Then you will have to be more careful in future.

GEORGE. I certainly will.

TAPEWORTH. I, too, must make that resolution.

GEORGE. What resolution?

TAPEWORTH. To be more careful. To avoid temptation, and resist the voice of Evil. Tonight, Mr Seegar, I have sold my soul. I entered into the temple of Bacchus and here I am before you, degraded and debauched, with vine leaves in my hair. Do you mind if I sit?

GEORGE. No, carry on.

(TAPEWORTH *sits in the armchair above the fireplace*)

TAPEWORTH. Thank you. You are very kind and this chair is very comfortable. (*He puts his head back on the cushion and closes his eyes*)

(GEORGE *crosses to the scullery door and opens it*)

GEORGE (*calling*) Albert!

ALBERT (*off; irritably*) Hello?

GEORGE. Come here a minute.

(ALBERT *appears in the doorway R*)

ALBERT. What is it?

GEORGE (*nodding his head towards Tapeworth*) Old Tapeworm.

ALBERT. Oh heck! I'd forgotten about him. I expect he'll be wanting his supper.

GEORGE. I don't think he'll want anything.

ALBERT. Why?

GEORGE. He's gone crackers.

ALBERT. Crackers?

GEORGE. Yes, he thinks he's got leaves in his hair. I don't know what he's been up to, but he's in a very peculiar mood.

ALBERT. Well, he's got a very peculiar job to start off with. Who's he been interviewing today? The directors or the strike leaders?

GEORGE. I don't know.

ALBERT. Hasn't he told you where he's been?

GEORGE. He mentioned a temple.

ALBERT. A what?

GEORGE. Says he's lost his soul there. Look, I think you ought to pack this lodger lark of yours up. We shan't be safe in our beds with dangerous lunatics and loose women hanging about the place.

ALBERT. Loose women?

GEORGE. Yes. (*Nodding at the scullery door*) Those two in there.

ALBERT. Mrs Flannel's all right.

GEORGE. Well, I can't say the same for her daughter. If old Tapeworth hadn't come in just now, I'd have had to shout for help.

ALBERT. Get away. You weren't in any danger when I came in here a few minutes ago. In fact, you seemed to be enjoying yourself.

GEORGE. I was until Elsie left. It was all a bit of fun up to then. But after she'd gone, Rosie started on me in earnest. We're going to get ourselves into a proper mess if we're not careful.

ALBERT. Well, let's deal with one thing at a time. Right now, number one priority's over there. Come on, let's see if we can get a bit of sense out of him.

(ALBERT *and* GEORGE *approach Tapeworth warily. He appears to be asleep.* ALBERT, R *of the armchair, bends over and peers at him closely.* TAPEWORTH *snores suddenly, and breathes out heavily*)

ALBERT. Phew!

GEORGE (*moving behind the armchair and to the* L *of it*) What's up?

ALBERT. Whisky. He's not balmy—he's drunk.

GEORGE. I don't believe it. Old Tapeworm hitting the bottle's about as improbable as your Clara winning a beauty contest.

ALBERT. Now, now, George. There's no need for that. She's not your mother-in-law yet, remember.

GEORGE. She never will be, either, if she walks in here and finds out what's going on. You won't be her husband for long, either.

ALBERT. We'd better get him upstairs as quick as we can.

(TAPEWORTH *snores again and breathes out heavily*)

Foo! If you struck a match now he'd go up like a hydrogen bomb.

GEORGE. What do we do? Carry him?

ALBERT (*sarcastically*) No, we put skates on his feet and push him.

GEORGE. I mean, wouldn't it be easier to wake him up and get him to go upstairs under his own steam.

ALBERT (*doubtfully*) We can try if you like. But from my experience once they're out like this, they're out for the night.

GEORGE (*shaking Tapeworth gently*) Mr Tapeworth!

(TAPEWORTH *remains unconscious*)

ALBERT. Come here, let me have a try. (*Shouting*) Hoy! Mr Tapeworth. (*He shakes him roughly*)

(TAPEWORTH *remains unconscious*)

By Gow! Have you felt him? He's wetter outside than he is in.

GEORGE. I know. He's been out in the rain.

ALBERT. I didn't suppose he'd been trying to swim the Channel. (*Shouting*) Mr Tapeworth!

(TAPEWORTH *remains unconscious*)

It's no good, we'll have to carry him. Get hold of his legs.

(GEORGE *lifts his legs.* TAPEWORTH *slides down into the chair.* ALBERT *stretches over the back of the chair to get hold of Tapeworth's shoulders but is unable to reach. He freezes suddenly, a look of apprehension coming over his face*)

GEORGE. What's up?

ALBERT. Me braces have gone.

(GEORGE *releases Tapeworth's legs.* TAPEWORTH *slides off the chair into a sitting position on the floor, still clutching his brief-case.* GEORGE *moves behind Albert and lifts the back of his jacket*)

GEORGE. It's not your braces, it's your buttons.

ALBERT. A fine thing to happen. Next thing I'll be losing my trousers.

GEORGE. If you've got a needle and cotton, I could stitch them on for you.

ALBERT. No time for that.

GEORGE. Well, hang on a minute. I'll get a safety-pin. I saw one on the mantelpiece. (*Moving to the mantelpiece and getting a safety-pin*) It'll only be temporary, mind you.

ALBERT. That's all right. I'll get Mrs Flannel to conduct permanent repairs later.

(GEORGE *pins Albert's trousers to his braces*)

GEORGE. There!

ALBERT. Thanks. Now I think if we move the chair, I can get hold of his top end without a lot of bending.

(GEORGE *pulls the armchair up stage.* TAPEWORTH *starts to fall backwards*)

(*He nips smartly in, catches him under the armpits and hoists him partly upright*) Well, go on, get hold of his legs. I can't support him like this all night.

(GEORGE *runs round, catches hold of Tapeworth's legs and hoists them up so quickly that* ALBERT *loses his balance and flops into the chair with* TAPEWORTH *on top of him.*
MRS FLANNEL *enters* R)

MRS FLANNEL (*stopping short*)　Oh, I'm sorry, I thought Mr Hellewell was in here.

ALBERT (*in a muffled voice*)　I am!

MRS FLANNEL (*crossing to the chair*)　Albert Hellewell, whatever are you doing down there?

ALBERT.　Playing hide and seek. What do you think?

MRS FLANNEL (*to George; laughing*)　Oh, he's a proper caution he is and no mistake.

ALBERT.　For heaven's sake get him off or I'll smother.

MRS FLANNEL (*to George*)　What happened?

GEORGE.　Old Tapeworth came in tight and flaked out. We were trying to carry him to bed.

ALBERT.　Never mind explanations. Get him off quick or you'll be carrying me to hospital.

(MRS FLANNEL *and* GEORGE *hoist Tapeworth up sufficiently to allow Albert to escape. They then release him and he flops back into the chair*)

(*Turning on George*)　A fine help you are! Now we're back where we started.

MRS FLANNEL.　Why don't you wake him up, and let him walk upstairs by himself.

ALBERT.　We've tried that.

MRS FLANNEL.　How did you go about it?

ALBERT.　We shook him a bit and shouted at him.

MRS FLANNEL.　That's no good.

ALBERT.　Then perhaps you could suggest something better.

MRS FLANNEL.　Certainly. I'll give him the treatment I used to give Joe if you like. It never failed in all the twenty years I was married to him.

ALBERT.　Carry on then. He's all yours.

MRS FLANNEL (*leaning over Tapeworth and slapping his face*)　Come on now, wakey, wakey.

(TAPEWORTH *remains unconscious*)

ALBERT.　It doesn't seem a very effective sort of treatment to me.

MRS FLANNEL.　I haven't started yet. (*To George*) Pass me that bottle.

(GEORGE *goes to the table and hands her the empty beer bottle.* MRS FLANNEL *holds the open neck under Tapeworth's nose.* TAPEWORTH *stirs slightly*)

That's right, pull yourself together. You can't sleep in a chair all night. (*To Albert*) He's coming round. (*She hands the bottle back to George, lifts one of Tapeworth's legs, rolls back the trouser bottom and pulls one of the hairs out of his leg*)

(TAPEWORTH *sits up with a jerk and opens his eyes*)

That never fails.

TAPEWORTH. Goodness, gracious me! Wherever am I?

GEORGE. You're all right, Mr Tapeworth. Just take things easy. You fell asleep, that's all.

TAPEWORTH. Oh, yes, I remember. How very unsociable of me. I must apologize for such churlish behaviour.

MRS FLANNEL. He'll be all right now. Keep him talking while I make him some black coffee. And get his wet things off him, or he'll be catching double pneumonia. (*She crosses to the door* R *and pauses*) Oh, I nearly forgot what I came in for, have you got such a thing as a needle and cotton, Albert? I've a little repair job to do for my daughter.

ALBERT. Try Clara's work-basket. It's on the top shelf of the cupboard in the scullery.

MRS FLANNEL. Thanks.

ALBERT. And if you've got a moment later on, I'd be glad if you'd do a little repair job for me as well.

MRS FLANNEL. Anything to oblige. As long as it doesn't take all night.

(MRS FLANNEL *exits* R)

ALBERT (*to Tapeworth*) Now then, Mr Tapeworth, how are you feeling?

TAPEWORTH. Ashamed, Mr Hellewell. Utterly ashamed.

ALBERT. There's no need to feel like that.

TAPEWORTH. Oh, but there is. I have brought degradation to your home.

ALBERT. Nay, I wouldn't say that. We all take a drop too much once in a while.

TAPEWORTH. No, we don't, Mr Hellewell. At least, I never have before.

ALBERT. You mean you're teetotal?

TAPEWORTH. I was, up to this evening. Goodness knows what will happen if mother ever finds out that strong drink has at last passed my lips.

ALBERT. How did it happen?

TAPEWORTH. I accepted the hospitality of the gentleman I have been interviewing all afternoon. For obvious reasons I cannot give his name.

ALBERT. No need to. Anyone who could get you into a state like that must be on an expense account. That narrows the field a bit. Where did you go?

TAPEWORTH. A place called the *Trocadero*.

ALBERT (*to George*) Obviously one of the directors. If he'd been with the strike committee he'd have finished up at the *Green Dragon*. (*To Tapeworth*) What happened when you got there?

TAPEWORTH. We had a meal, and some drinks, which he assured me were completely innocuous. After I'd unwittingly taken two I realized they were nothing of the sort. But by that time old Bacchus had me firmly in his grip, and I was unable to resist the further drinks that were offered.

ALBERT. You mean he forced you to drink against your will?

TAPEWORTH. Who?

ALBERT. This fellow Backhouse.

TAPEWORTH. Backhouse?

ALBERT. The chap who took you to the *Trocadero*.

TAPEWORTH. That wasn't Backhouse.

ALBERT. Then who was it?

TAPEWORTH. Sanderson.

GEORGE. The managing director.

ALBERT. So there were two of 'em?

TAPEWORTH. Two of who?

ALBERT. Two of 'em took you to dinner.

TAPEWORTH. No, only one.

ALBERT. But if Sanderson took you to the *Trocadero*, and Backhouse forced you to drink when you didn't want to . . .

TAPEWORTH. No, no, no, Mr Hellewell, no-one forced me to drink against my will . . .

ALBERT. But you just said they did.

TAPEWORTH. When?

ALBERT. Just now. You said old Backhouse had you in his clutches . . .

TAPEWORTH. I said old Bacchus had me in his grip.

ALBERT. That's the fellow I've been trying to get at.

TAPEWORTH. But he wasn't there.

ALBERT (*incredulous*) He wasn't there?

TAPEWORTH. You misunderstand, I was speaking in metaphor.

ALBERT. Then try speaking in English and perhaps we'll understand you.

TAPEWORTH. I was referring to the Roman god of wine.

ALBERT. Don't tell me he was there an' all.

TAPEWORTH. Who?

ALBERT. Nay, dammit, I give up. (*To George*) Do you know what he's talking about?

GEORGE. Yes.

ALBERT. Then why didn't you say so.

GEORGE. I never got chance. All Mr Tapeworth means is that after he'd had a couple of glasses of wallop, he couldn't say no to a third. Isn't that so?

TAPEWORTH. Quite correct, Mr Seegar. I have fallen into temptation and been filled with corruption.

ALBERT. And I suppose you'll be telling us in a minute that corruption's the Roman name for Johnnie Walker.

TAPEWORTH. No, Mr Hellewell. I mean I have accepted hospitality from one of the sides involved in the dispute. I cannot, therefore, be said to be an impartial assessor. If what I have done becomes known, my integrity will be in doubt and I shall probably lose my job.

GEORGE. But no-one can doubt your integrity if you prove that this evening hasn't influenced your decision in any way.

TAPEWORTH. Ah, if only I could do that.

GEORGE. You can.

TAPEWORTH. How?

GEORGE. By reporting in favour of the other side.

TAPEWORTH (*appalled*) The strikers?

GEORGE. Yes.

TAPEWORTH. Oh, I couldn't do that.

GEORGE. Why not?

TAPEWORTH. Well, for one thing, I've already made my report to higher authority recommending just the opposite.

GEORGE. Then change it.

TAPEWORTH. I can't, I posted it—(*suddenly doubtful*) or did I?

GEORGE. Aren't you sure?

TAPEWORTH. Well, I intended posting it on the way to the *Trocadero*, but we took a taxi so I couldn't have done. I wonder if I put it back in my brief-case.

GEORGE (*picking up his brief-case and going up stage of the table*) Well, let's find out. (*He opens the brief-case, pulls out a sheaf of papers, divides them roughly into two and hands one half to Albert*) Have a look through that lot.

(ALBERT *moves to* L *of the table*)

TAPEWORTH (*rising; distressed*) Please, Mr Seegar—that brief-case is private property . . .

ALBERT (*moving to the dresser with the papers*) That's all right, Mr Tapeworth, you're among friends.

TAPEWORTH. But the documents are confidential.

GEORGE. I'll say, listen to this. (*Reading from a document and moving* c) "My dearest Benjamin, As I sit here, typing your report to the Minister, my fingers long to caress your face instead of the keys of my typewriter."

(TAPEWORTH *snatches it from him*)

ALBERT (*pretending to be shocked*) Mr Tapeworth! I bet your mother doesn't know about that, does she?

TAPEWORTH. It's only a memo from one of the typists.

ALBERT (*moving down to* L *of the table*) By Gow, you get a lot more fun in your office than we do in the welding shop. And I allus thought Civil Servants did nowt but drink tea.

TAPEWORTH. It was written by a rather backward girl in the typing pool.

GEORGE. She doesn't sound very backward to me.

TAPEWORTH. I was referring to her mental rather than her physical properties, Mr Seegar. I need hardly add that her feelings were not reciprocated.

ALBERT. I should hope not.

TAPEWORTH. I did everything I could to discourage her, but to no avail. For six months she pinned one of those things to every report I had typed. Each one was more suggestive than its predecessor. In the end I could hardly look her in the face.

GEORGE. I'll bet you couldn't.

(ALBERT *flicks through his papers*)

What are you doing?

ALBERT. Looking for the rest of the set.

TAPEWORTH. There's no more, Mr Hellewell. I destroyed them all after one went through to the Minister by mistake.

ALBERT. I bet that shook him.

TAPEWORTH. It did indeed. He thought I'd written it.

GEORGE. Go on! What did you do?

TAPEWORTH. Told him the truth. He was most understanding. He transferred the girl to his own staff the following week.

ALBERT (*searching through the papers*) Hello, what's this?

TAPEWORTH. Not another one?

ALBERT. No. (*Reading*) "Standing instructions for Sit Down Strikes." We're getting warm. Here we are. (*Reading*) "Strike at Sanderson Brothers. Report and recommendation."

GEORGE (*taking it from him*) That's it.

TAPEWORTH. I don't think you ought to read it, Mr Seegar—really I don't—it's most confidential . . .

GEORGE. It can't be any worse than what we've read already.

TAPEWORTH. You don't understand. No-one but the Minister is supposed to read that report . . .

GEORGE. I'll say nothing, and you know how to keep your mouth shut, don't you, Albert?

ALBERT. I should do, after twenty-five years of matrimony.

TAPEWORTH. But that's not the point . . .

GEORGE (*scanning the report*) Now then, I think we can deal with this fairly quickly. By just altering a word or two here and there and cutting out the last paragraph, we can change the whole meaning. Just sit over here a minute, Mr Tapeworth. (*He moves to the chair behind the table and pulls it out*)

TAPEWORTH (*crossing to the table and sitting*) I don't really think I ought, Mr Seegar. I shall be out of order if I do.

GEORGE (R *of Tapeworth*) You'll be out of work if you don't.

(*Taking Tapeworth's pen out of his waistcoat pocket and handing it to him*)
Now then, just alter the bits I tell you to.

(MRS FLANNEL *enters* R. *She carries a cup of coffee*)

MRS FLANNEL (*moving behind the chair* L *of the table; to Albert*) Here
we are, this should do the trick . . .

(ALBERT *takes the cup from her*)

(*Noticing Tapeworth*) Ah, the patient seems to be recovering.
ALBERT. He is indeed—thanks to you.
MRS FLANNEL. What's he doing?
ALBERT. Writing to his mother.
MRS FLANNEL (*surprised*) Writing to his mother?
ALBERT (*confidentially*) He does it every night.
MRS FLANNEL. Really?
ALBERT. Oh, yes. Very dutiful he is to his mother. He's having
a bit of difficulty tonight, though, so he's asked George to give him
a hand.
MRS FLANNEL. Oh, why?
ALBERT (*winking at her*) Well, the table keeps turning over so he's
asked George to hold it down for him.
MRS FLANNEL. Oh, I see. Well, I'll leave you to it. I've got to
get back to me bit of sewing. (*Moving to the scullery door*) Don't forget
to see he takes his wet things off before he goes to bed.
ALBERT. I won't.

(MRS FLANNEL *exits* R)

(*Moving to* L *of Tapeworth*) Here you are, Mr Tapeworth. (*He puts the
cup of coffee beside him*) Get that inside you. It'll warm you up.
TAPEWORTH. Thank you, Mr Hellewell, you are most kind. (*To
George*) Have we finished?
GEORGE. Just cross that last paragraph out and initial it.

(TAPEWORTH *does so*)

TAPEWORTH. There. How's that?
GEORGE. Fine. Now there's no danger to you getting the sack.
It's a good job you've got friends to look after you.
TAPEWORTH. I'm most grateful.
ALBERT. Now just drink your coffee and we'll take you up to
beddy-byes.
TAPEWORTH. To where?
ALBERT. Upstairs. To sleep it off. You'll feel better in the morn-
ing.
TAPEWORTH (*solemnly*) I'm quite capable of going upstairs by
myself. (*He drinks the coffee*)
ALBERT. That's fine. But before you do we'd better get your
clothes off.
TAPEWORTH (*in alarm*) Get my clothes off?

GEORGE. Well, at least your jacket and trousers. They're wet through.

TAPEWORTH (*rising*) Oh, now wait a minute, Mr Seegar . . .

ALBERT. It's all right. We'll dry them off for you.

GEORGE. It won't take a second. (*He takes off Tapeworth's jacket*)

TAPEWORTH (*protesting*) Really! This is most embarrassing . . .

ALBERT. Now the trousers.

TAPEWORTH. No! No! You mustn't take my trousers off, Mr Hellewell. Modesty forbids it. (*Moving quickly to the fireplace*) Mother always warned me about taking my trousers off before strangers.

ALBERT (*moving to Tapeworth*) We're not strangers. We're your friends. Aren't we, George?

GEORGE. That's right.

ALBERT. You'll be quite safe. The girls are in the scullery. (*He starts to undo Tapeworth's trousers*)

TAPEWORTH (*moving up stage, L of the armchair above the fireplace, to the door L; in panic*) No, really, Mr Hellewell, I cannot expose my dignity to such treatment.

ALBERT. We're not asking you to expose anything. Anyway, you've got your underpants on.

TAPEWORTH. You don't understand. Some things are inviolate.

ALBERT. Mine are in pink. But I'm not ashamed of it. Clara ran 'em up out of some old curtains.

TAPEWORTH. Please, Mr Hellewell—do not force me to disrobe further—let me retire unmolested—please . . .

ALBERT. All right, if you feel as strongly about it as all that. But if I was you I'd put me health first. There's no knowing what you might catch through wearing wet pants.

TAPEWORTH. That, Mr Hellewell, is a risk I took as a baby and survived. (*Dignified but still unsteady*) Good night.

(TAPEWORTH *exits* L)

GEORGE ⎱
ALBERT ⎰ Good night.

GEORGE. Do you think he'll make it?

(*There is a crash off* L)

ALBERT. Eventually. We'll go up in a few minutes and see if he's all right.

GEORGE (*putting Tapeworth's jacket on the table and picking up the report*) I reckon that's the best night's work we've done for some time. (*He folds it up*) I told you if we played our cards right we could use him to help the Cause.

ALBERT. The strike's not over yet.

GEORGE. It will be when this report goes through. I'd better get it into the post. Have you got an envelope?

ALBERT. Have a look in the dresser.

(GEORGE *starts to search in the dresser.* ALBERT *crosses to the table and picks up Tapeworth's jacket. He takes the chair from* L *of the table to the fireplace and hangs the jacket on the back of it to dry.*

Mrs Flannel *enters* R *with a needle and cotton*)

Mrs Flannel. Have you finished with the cup?

Albert. It's on the table. It did the trick all right. He's gone off like a lamb.

Mrs Flannel. I'm glad to hear it. All he'll need now is a couple of Alkaseltzers in the morning. (*Holding up needle and cotton*) I've finished my sewing. (*Moving to* c) Where's the little job you wanted me to do for you.

Albert (*lifting his jacket*) Here. I've lost the buttons off me pants.

George. I can't find one, Albert.

Albert. Try the cupboard in the scullery.

George. Right.

(George *exits* R)

Mrs Flannel. Have you got the buttons?

Albert. I think so. (*Moving to Mrs Flannel. Feeling in his pockets*) Ah yes, here we are. (*He produces them*)

Mrs Flannel (*taking them*) Thanks. It's going to be a bit awkward with your trousers on.

Albert (*in alarm*) Eh?

Mrs Flannel. But I'll manage. Take your jacket off and bend over the table.

(Albert *takes his jacket off, goes to the table and bends over it*)

I'll try not to prick you. (*She threads the needle through his trousers, and is about to insert it through the button when she drops it down inside of his trousers*)

Mrs Flannel. Well! That's done it and no mistake.

Albert. What has?

Mrs Flannel. I've dropped the button.

Albert. Well, pick it up.

Mrs Flannel. I can't, it's gone down the inside of your pants. You'd better jump about 'til it falls out.

(Albert *jumps about. The button doesn't appear*)

Albert. It's got stuck somewhere. (*He tries unsuccessfully to retrieve it by putting his hand down the back of his trousers*)

Mrs Flannel (*impatiently*) Oh, come here. (*She is about to put her hand down the back of his trousers*)

(Clara *and* Elsie *enter up* L)

Clara. Well!

Albert. Clara!

Clara. What's going on?

Albert. Nothing, love. Nothing at all. (*Weakly*) She was only—

(*he takes a step forward and almost loses his trousers*) helping me to find me button.

CLARA. It looks like it.

ALBERT. There's really quite a simple explanation . . .

(GEORGE *enters hurriedly* R. *He stops short at the sight of Elsie and Clara and retreats to the door* R.

ROSIE *enters* R, *dressed in her stage costume*)

ROSIE. Georgie!

GEORGE. Excuse me. (*He crosses the room quickly to the door* L, *and opens it*)

(TAPEWORTH *enters* L, *carrying his trousers over his arm*)

TAPEWORTH. You were quite right, Mr Hellewell. Health before modesty. (*He suddenly realizes that there are members of the fair sex present*) Good gracious me!

He retreats in panic to the door L, *trying to shield himself with his trousers as—*

the CURTAIN *falls*

ACT III

SCENE—*The same. Early the following morning.*

When the CURTAIN *rises, the camp bed on which* ALBERT *has spent the night is* C, *running up and down the stage so that anyone lying in it faces the audience. Albert's pyjamas are on the bed and his dressing-gown is on the armchair below the window. There is an official letter, addressed to Tapeworth, propped up on the mantelshelf. The armchair below the fireplace is now set in front of the fireplace.* ALBERT *is standing on this armchair, looking into the mirror above the mantelpiece. He is shaving with a cutthroat razor. He is wearing shirt and trousers and has a towel tucked under his chin.* CLARA *enters up* L. *She carries a suitcase which she puts down in the lobby.* ALBERT, *intent on his shaving, does not notice her.*

CLARA (*moving to* C) Well, I didn't expect to find you up at this time.

ALBERT (*jumping and looking round*) Eh?

CLARA. Or haven't you been to bed yet?

ALBERT (*seeing her*) Oh, it's you, Clara.

CLARA. Who did you think it was? The police? Coming to raid the place?

ALBERT. No, I didn't. Anyway, if it had been, they wouldn't have crept up quietly behind me like that. Not when I was shaving. You want to be careful. I might have cut me throat through shock.

CLARA. After what I saw here last night, I wonder you haven't already cut it through shame.

ALBERT (*climbing down from the armchair*) Now, look here, Clara, if you want to create trouble . . .

CLARA. Me? Create trouble? I'll have you know that's the one thing I've spent my life trying to avoid.

ALBERT (*pushing the armchair back into position below the fireplace*) Well, I can't say it's been very obvious.

CLARA. Do you wonder? When I've got a husband who spends his time carrying on with loose women.

ALBERT. I've told you before I wasn't carrying on.

CLARA. Oh, I don't expect you to admit it. It's not in your nature to admit anything. The only good thing I can say about last night is that our Elsie's had her eyes opened in time. Not like her mother who's seen the red light too late. If I'd thought for one moment, that night you proposed to me behind the gas works, that things were going to turn out like this . . . (*She is beginning to get a little tearful*)

ALBERT. Now, now, Clara, there's no need to take on. I explained everything to you. Mrs Flannel and her daughter are only here in a business capacity.

CLARA. You don't have to tell me that. From what I saw last night it was only too obvious.

ALBERT (*wiping his face with the towel*) Well, they wouldn't have been here at all if you hadn't put that advert in the paper.

CLARA. Oh, so I'm to blame now, am I? I'm responsible for my husband's misconduct?

ALBERT (*putting the razor on the mantelpiece*) Look it's no good going on like this. If you won't believe my story there's nothing more I can do about it.

CLARA. Oh, yes, there is.

ALBERT. What?

CLARA. You can get rid of her. And her daughter.

ALBERT. When?

CLARA. Today. That'll prove whether she means anything to you or not.

ALBERT. I can't.

CLARA. Why?

ALBERT. I'd have to return her money. She's paid me a week in advance.

CLARA. Oh, so money comes before me now, does it?

ALBERT. Don't talk so daft. I couldn't give her it back if I wanted to. I've spent it.

CLARA. Drunk it, you mean.

ALBERT (*on his dignity*) That, Clara Hellewell, is not only untrue but quite unjustified.

CLARA. It's no good getting all hoity-toity with me. You know very well that every quid you get burns a hole in your pocket till it finds its way into the till of the *Green Dragon*. (*She searches in her handbag and brings out three one-pound notes*) Here, how much do you want to get rid of her?

ALBERT. Nothing.

CLARA. What do you mean—nothing?

ALBERT. I don't want to get rid of her. She can stay here as long as she likes.

CLARA (*astounded*) She can what?

ALBERT. She can stay here.

CLARA (*tight-lipped*) So!

ALBERT. Well, there'd be no sense in getting rid of someone who cooks me meals, cleans me shoes and sews me buttons on, and pays me into the bargain for the privilege of doing it.

CLARA. You mean you don't want me back?

ALBERT. You can come back if you want.

CLARA. As another member of your harem, I suppose?

ALBERT. No, as another paying guest.

CLARA. As a what?

ALBERT. On special terms, of course. A quid a week. I couldn't charge much more for a hammock in the scullery.

CLARA. Albert Hellewell. Do you know what you're saying?

ALBERT. Aye, I'm dictating terms to you like you did to me two days ago.

CLARA. I don't think I can be hearing you right.

ALBERT. Then you'd better get yourself an ear trumpet. Or shall I say it all again a bit louder?

CLARA (*grimly*) I think you've said quite enough already.

ALBERT. Then we know where we stand, don't we?

CLARA. We do, indeed. (*She goes to the lobby and picks up her suitcase*)

ALBERT. If you decide to take the scullery, I'll reduce the price to fifteen shillings. As a special concession, seeing it's you.

50 CLARA (*exploding*) Oh! (*She turns to go*)

(GEORGE *enters up* L. GEORGE *and* CLARA *almost collide*)

GEORGE (*brightly*) Good morning.

CLARA. Good-bye.

(CLARA *exits up* L, *slamming the door behind her*)

GEORGE (*moving to* R *of the armchair above the fireplace*) Well? What was all that about?

ALBERT (*sitting in the armchair above the fireplace*) By Gow, George, you've just missed a treat, you have indeed.

GEORGE. Oh!

ALBERT. I can't remember when I've enjoyed meself so much. (*Laughing*) You should have seen her face, George. Speechless she was. She came in here, a flag of truce in her hand, almost begging me to take her back. She even offered me money to get rid of Mrs Flannel, and do you know what I did? (*He is laughing heartily at his own cleverness*) You'll never guess. I offered her the scullery at a quid a week. (*He can hardly go on for laughing*) And then I reduced it to fifteen shillings as a special concession. I could hardly keep me face straight. But Gow, we're winning now, George. The enemy's on the run and no mistake.

GEORGE (*moving to the dresser; doubtfully*) I hope you're right.

ALBERT (*rising; suddenly sobering up*) Hey, what's up? You seem to have lost your enthusiasm all of a sudden.

GEORGE (*turning*) I have. I started losing it last night when Rosie started showing too much.

ALBERT. Well, I admit her costume was a bit brief, but I didn't know she'd been . . .

GEORGE. I'm talking about enthusiasm.

ALBERT. Oh.

GEORGE. I had my suspicions then, but now they've been confirmed.

ALBERT. What are you talking about?

GEORGE. Rosie and her mother. They're dangerous.

ALBERT. Get away. They're no more dangerous than most

women. You've just got to know how to handle them. It's like playing with matches. If you hold the right end then you don't get burnt.

GEORGE. And if you play with matches in the dark, you're just as likely to get hold of the wrong end as you are the right. That's what's been happening to us. We've been in the dark, you and I, Albert.

ALBERT. Look, for heaven's sake stop talking in riddles and tell me what you're getting at.

GEORGE. I've just been talking to Bill Arkwright.

ALBERT. The fellow who works the lights at the Palace?

GEORGE. That's right. He knows our Rosie and her mother.

ALBERT. Well, I'm not surprised at that. They're in a show there next week, aren't they?

GEORGE. No, they're not. They were in a show there a fortnight before Christmas. It flopped, and they haven't worked since.

ALBERT. Well?

GEORGE. For the past four months they've been staying at Bill's place for nothing.

ALBERT. You mean he's a relative of theirs.

GEORGE. Relative, my foot. His wife runs a boarding-house. Or did. I don't know what she's doing now. She left him at the end of February.

ALBERT. Why?

GEORGE. Oh, use your loaf. It's quite simple. Rosie and her mother are on their uppers, right?

ALBERT. Right.

GEORGE. So they get themselves fixed up nicely in lodgings, together with all their other pals from the show.

ALBERT (*pointing to the ceiling*) Yvonne and Estelle?

GEORGE. And Bert Wheatly. And any others who happen to be around with no place to go. They pay a week's rent in advance and then they get to work. By the end of the first week they're dug in so well that no-one has the heart to ask them for their following week's rent. At the end of a fortnight, they're playing the landlord off against his wife and they finish up by driving her out and taking over without paying another cent. They're half way there already with us. No womenfolk to contend with. Bill said he had a helluva time getting rid of them. He had to get the police in. So now you can see what sort of a mess you've got us both into.

ALBERT. Me?

GEORGE. Yes. You and your lodgers. It just goes to show where greed gets you. If you hadn't turned capitalist . . .

ALBERT (*taking a pace towards him*) Now wait a bit, George . . .

GEORGE. However, I don't suppose there's any point in crying over spilt milk. We'll just have to think of a way to get rid of them.

ALBERT (*sitting on the camp bed*) That's easy. We'll tell 'em to go at the end of the week.

GEORGE. By which time they'll have convinced Elsie and Clara that what they saw here last night really was something. If we do it that way we've lost Elsie and Clara for good. No, we've got to be more subtle. I've already started one line of action . . .

ALBERT. What?

GEORGE. There's no time to explain now. You'll find out later. What we want at the moment is a second string to our bow. Something else, just to make sure. Something that'll drive them out immediately.

ALBERT. What?

GEORGE. I don't know. Haven't you any ideas?

ALBERT. Well, short of setting fire to the place . . .

GEORGE. Too risky. We'd probably finish up in gaol for arson.

(*There is a pause*)

ALBERT. A couple of years ago there were some folk in Henry Street who had to get out of their house due to a plague of ants . . .

GEORGE (*moving* C, *behind the camp bed*) That's it!

ALBERT. What? Ants?

GEORGE. No—plague, illness, disease. You're not feeling well. You've got a splitting headache and spots on the chest.

ALBERT. Don't talk so daft. I've never felt better in me life.

GEORGE. They won't know that. Here, get into your pyjamas. (*He picks them up from the bed*)

ALBERT. Get into me what? Now wait a bit, George . . .

GEORGE. There's no time to argue. They'll be down in a minute. What you've got to do is to convince them that you're suffering from something infectious and unpleasant . . .

ALBERT. Why me?

GEORGE. You're better at malingering than I am.

ALBERT. I'm what?

GEORGE. And in any case your bed's right here in the sitting-room. Now then, we'll have to make you look ill. (*He moves to the mantelpiece and takes down a small trinket box which he opens*)

ALBERT. Can't I look ill without getting undressed.

GEORGE. No. (*Taking a powder-puff out of the box*) You've got to be convincing. For a start we'll get rid of your healthy complexion. (*He returns to the bed and powders Albert's face*)

ALBERT. Hey, what the heck are you playing at?

GEORGE. It's all right. It's only Elsie's face powder. And now for some spots. (*He hoists Albert to his feet, opens his shirt and starts to cover his chest with red marks from a lipstick which he has taken out of the box*)

ALBERT. Nay, dammit all, George, there's a limit to everything . . .

GEORGE. Take it easy, it's only lipstick. (*Standing back and admiring his work*) There, I think that'll do. Now get into your pyjamas and pop into bed quick.

(ALBERT *starts to undress.*
    The sound of footsteps approaching is heard off L)

ALBERT. They're here. We're too late.

GEORGE. Into the scullery—quick. (*He propels Albert to the door* R)
Come back in a few minutes and give it all you've got.

(ALBERT *is pushed off* R *by* GEORGE.

TAPEWORTH *enters* L. *He is very pale and suffering from a bad hang-over. He is without his glasses. He walks gingerly into the room and sits carefully in the armchair above the fireplace*)

GEORGE (*crossing to* R *of Tapeworth*) Hello, what's the matter with
you?

TAPEWORTH. I'm not very well, Mr Seegar. In fact, I think I'm
going to die.

GEORGE (*cheerfully*) Well, we all come to it sooner or later.

TAPEWORTH. Indeed, we do. I had hoped to continue my
existence a little longer, but I fear my demise is imminent.

GEORGE (*looking at him in astonishment*) You meant that, didn't you?

TAPEWORTH. Of course I did, Mr Seegar. The symptoms are all
there. I've been looking them up in Black's *Medical Dictionary*.
There's no doubt about it. I'm suffering from an impending attack
of encephalitis.

GEORGE. Of what?

TAPEWORTH. Encephalitis. It starts with a splitting headache,
fits of giddiness, nausea . . .

GEORGE. Sounds more like a hangover to me.

TAPEWORTH. A hangover?

GEORGE. That's right.

TAPEWORTH. Do you really think so?

GEORGE. Well, I wouldn't be certain. But I think it's very likely,
in view of the state you were in last night.

TAPEWORTH (*apprehensive*) Oh, dear. Did I—I mean had I—I
mean, was I intoxicated?

GEORGE. Just a bit.

TAPEWORTH. I hope I didn't do anything to be ashamed of.

GEORGE. I don't think you need worry. I imagine we've all seen
people in their underwear before. Even the females who were present.

TAPEWORTH (*horrified*) Mr Seegar, you don't mean I displayed
my underwear in front of ladies!

GEORGE. Well, not for very long, just momentarily.

TAPEWORTH. Good gracious me, how terrible. If mother ever
finds out about this . . .

GEORGE. It's very unlikely, so I shouldn't worry. How about
some breakfast?

TAPEWORTH (*shuddering at the thought*) No, thank you. I couldn't.
Thanks all the same. Oh dear, they were my darned ones, too.

GEORGE (*moving to the fireplace and taking a letter from the mantelpiece*)
There's a letter here for you.

TAPEWORTH. A letter? For me?

GEORGE (*looking at the envelope*) That's what it says. It's re-addressed from the *Midland Hotel*. Looks as though the tax people have caught up with you. It's O.H.M.S. (*He hands it to him*)

TAPEWORTH (*taking the letter and opening it*) Thank you. (*Looking at it*) It's from my headquarters. I wonder if you'd be so good as to read it. I've left my glasses upstairs.

GEORGE (*taking it and reading*) It's headed "Subsistence allowance".

TAPEWORTH (*alarmed*) Subsistence—oh dear. Who's it signed by?

GEORGE. I can't make out the signature, but it's got ABtwo under it.

TAPEWORTH (*in consternation*) ABtwo? Accounts Branch. What does it say?

GEORGE (*reading*) "It has been brought to our notice that for the past twelve months you have been occupying cheap lodgings whilst engaged on outside duties. As you have consistently claimed for first class hotel accommodation over this period you are requested to report to Room two-o-seven-o at two p.m. on the seventh of May to appear before the Investigation Committee to justify and explain your conduct." Is it true?

TAPEWORTH (*very quietly*) Yes, I'm afraid so. It's the end of my career, Mr Seegar. I shall have to resign.

GEORGE. It's as serious as that?

TAPEWORTH. Yes. Does it say anything else?

GEORGE. There's a note pinned to it. (*Reading*) It says "Hell hath no fury . . ."

TAPEWORTH. Like a woman scorned. Well, that shows how they've found out, anyway. I don't know how I'm going to explain all this to mother—she'll never get over the disgrace.

(GEORGE *hands him the letter.* TAPEWORTH *takes it mechanically. He is very upset.*

ALBERT *enters* R. *He is wearing his pyjamas*)

ALBERT (*moving to the head of the camp bed, swaying and supporting himself on the furniture*) Oh . . . ! Oh . . . I do feel bad! . . . My head's splitting . . .

GEORGE (*crossing to Albert; under his breath*) Don't overdo it.

ALBERT (*to George*) Eh?

GEORGE (*to Albert*) I said, don't overdo it.

ALBERT (*to George; testily*) Well, you told me to give it all I'd got.

GEORGE (*to Albert; giving a quick glance at Tapeworth who is wholly engrossed with his own thoughts*) Yes, but not all at once. Spread it out a bit.

TAPEWORTH. Oh dear! Oh dear, oh dear!

ALBERT (*to George; in surprise*) What's up with him?

GEORGE (*to Albert*) A hangover.

ALBERT. Oh. I thought for a minute you'd got him to join in as well.

TAPEWORTH (*thinking aloud*) I shall have to take mother away from Stoke Poges. She'll never be able to hold her head up there again after this.

ALBERT (*to George*) What's he talking about?

GEORGE. He's been doing a fiddle over his allowance and they've found him out.

ALBERT. That's what happens when you start deceiving folk. Sooner or later they—(*Suddenly realizing it also applies to himself*) Look, George, I don't think we ought to go through with this.

GEORGE. We can't turn back now, it's too late.

ALBERT. It's all right for you . . .

GEORGE. Look, there's no time to argue. Get into bed.

(ROSIE *and* MRS FLANNEL *are heard off* L)

Quick, they're here.

(ALBERT *gets quickly into bed.* GEORGE *moves to* R *of the bed, gets hold of Albert's right wrist and pretends to be taking his pulse.*
MRS FLANNEL *and* ROSIE *enter* L)

MRS FLANNEL. Good morning. (*Stopping short*) Oh! Whatever's the matter?

GEORGE (*casually*) It's nothing. Just Albert. He's not feeling very well.

MRS FLANNEL. I knew it. (*She moves to* L *of the bed*)

ALBERT (*sitting up*) Eh?

(GEORGE *pushes him down*)

MRS FLANNEL. I knew something had happened the moment I got out of bed. In fact, I said to Rosie as I put my corsets on, "Rosie," I said, "my clairvoyance is working overtime this morning. Things aren't as they should be." Didn't I, love?

ROSIE (*moving below the dresser*) That's right, Mum, you did.

MRS FLANNEL. It's that tinned salmon I gave him for tea. I thought it was off.

TAPEWORTH (*to himself*) Oh dear, oh dear.

MRS FLANNEL. Mr Tapeworth! I didn't notice you sitting there. Are you in trouble, too?

TAPEWORTH. Terrible trouble.

MRS FLANNEL (*rolling up her sleeves*) Well, we'd better get to work on them. (*To George*) I don't suppose there's such a thing as a stomach pump in the house?

ALBERT (*sitting up in alarm*) A what?

GEORGE (*pushing him down again*) I doubt it.

MRS FLANNEL. Then we'll have to prepare an emetic . . .

ALBERT (*sitting up quickly*) Now look here . . .

(GEORGE *pushes him down again and puts the bedclothes over his head*)

MRS FLANNEL. Rosie, nip into the scullery and get two glasses of water.

Rosie (*moving to the door* R) Right, Mum.

Mrs Flannel. And see if you can find a packet of salt.

George. I think a raw egg with Worcester sauce would be more in Mr Tapeworth's line. He's only got a hangover.

Mrs Flannel (*sharply*) I'm well aware of that.

George. Oh, I thought you were going to give him salt and water.

Mrs Flannel. That's for Albert.

Albert (*disentangling himself from the bedclothes and sitting up*) I think I'm feeling a bit better.

(George *pushes him down again*)

Mrs Flannel. I'm giving Mr Tapeworth Alkaseltzer. I have some in my bag. Any objections?

George. No, I just thought . . .

Mrs Flannel. Leave the thinking to me, Mr Seegar.

Rosie (*coyly*) Can I get you a cup of tea while I'm in the scullery, Georgie?

Mrs Flannel. There's no time for that now, Rosie. You can give your sweetheart a cup of tea when we've got the crisis over.

Rosie. Rightio! (*She gives George a seductive smile*) Sweetheart!

(George *smiles wanly at Rosie.*
    Rosie *exits* R)

Mrs Flannel. What's his pulse?

George. Eh? (*Suddenly realizing he is still holding Albert's wrist*) Oh, his pulse? Um—(*wildly*) four hundred and twenty.

Mrs Flannel. What?

George. I mean, two hundred and forty.

Mrs Flannel. Come here. (*She gets hold of Albert's left wrist*) It's quite obvious you haven't had much experience at nursing, Mr Seegar. It's a good job this happened whilst I was here.

Albert (*sitting up*) I'm feeling a lot better now.

Mrs Flannel (*pushing him down*) You'll feel better still when I've finished with you.

George. Don't you think we ought to get the doctor?

Mrs Flannel. You don't need a doctor when you've got a F.A.N.Y.

Albert. A what?

Mrs Flannel. First Aid Nursing Yeomanry.

George. You?

Mrs Flannel. Over three years during the last war.

Albert (*to George*) Fine second string to your bow this has turned out to be.

George (*ignoring him; to Mrs Flannel*) I still think we ought to seek a doctor's opinion, Mrs Flannel.

Mrs Flannel. Are you doubting my ability to deal with a food poisoning case, Mr Seegar?

GEORGE. No, but it's just possible that Albert's got something more serious.

MRS FLANNEL. What, for example?

GEORGE. Well—er—typhoid.

MRS FLANNEL (*putting her hand on Albert's forehead*) No fever.

GEORGE. Then how about cholera?

MRS FLANNEL. He couldn't sit up if he'd got that.

GEORGE (*desperately*) Bubonic plague?

MRS FLANNEL. Unlikely. Anyway, it only occurs where there's rats.

ALBERT (*trying to back George up*) Oh, we've got one or two of them. I've seen 'em in the yard.

TAPEWORTH (*suddenly giving his attention to the conversation*) Rats?

ALBERT. Oh, yes. They come from Joe Popplewell's hen-run down the street. We sometimes get them in the house as well.

TAPEWORTH (*in alarm*) You mean this place is rat-infested?

ALBERT. Oh, I wouldn't say that. I've never seen more than half a dozen at a time.

TAPEWORTH (*horrified*) Half a dozen?

ALBERT. Well, you can't expect the *Savoy* for two pounds ten a week.

GEORGE. So it doesn't look as though we can rule out bubonic plague after all, Mrs Flannel.

TAPEWORTH (*scrambling to his feet; in great alarm*) Bubonic plague!

GEORGE. Yes, we think Albert's got a slight touch of it.

TAPEWORTH (*backing away to the door* L) Mercy on us!

MRS FLANNEL. There's no need to get excited, Mr Tapeworth.

ALBERT. No, they can cure anything these days with penicilin.

TAPEWORTH. But it's fatal, Mr Hellewell—absolutely fatal. According to B.M.D. (*He takes a handkerchief from his pocket*)

ALBERT. Who's B.M.D.?

TAPEWORTH. Black's *Medical Dictionary*. I've got a copy upstairs. I think I'd better go and look it up.

(TAPEWORTH *stumbles out* L, *holding the handkerchief to his face*)

MRS FLANNEL. Well, I hope you're satisfied. Scaring the pants off him. What's the idea, trying to make out you've got bubonic plague?

ALBERT (*innocently*) Haven't I?

MRS FLANNEL. Of course not. You wouldn't be conscious if you had. You know, I'm just beginning to wonder whether you've even got food poisoning.

GEORGE. Well, he's got something, that's certain.

MRS FLANNEL. It can't be anything serious. His pulse is normal and he's no temperature.

ALBERT. Well—er—maybe it's just a touch of nettlerash.

MRS FLANNEL. Nettlerash?

ALBERT. Or measles.

MRS FLANNEL. You'd have spots.

ALBERT. I have. (*He opens his jacket and displays his chest*) Hundreds of 'em!

MRS FLANNEL. Then why didn't you say so? (*Looking closely at his chest*) Goodness me. I've never seen spots like that before.

ALBERT. Horrible, aren't they?

MRS FLANNEL. Do they itch?

ALBERT (*scratching himself vigorously*) Something chronic.

(ROSIE *enters* R, *carrying two glasses of colourless liquid on a tray*)

ROSIE (*moving behind the table*) I could only find Epsom salt. But I don't suppose it'll matter. Up or down, you get the same result, don't you? (*She points to the glass on the* L) That's the water for Mr Tapeworth's Alkaseltzer. Oh, where's he gone? (*She puts the tray down on the table*)

MRS FLANNEL. Upstairs.

ROSIE. Shall I take it up to him?

MRS FLANNEL. You'll find the tablets in my bag.

(ROSIE *looks round for the bag*)

It's upstairs on the dressing-table.

ROSIE (*picking up the right-hand glass*) Right.

(ROSIE *goes out* L, *smiling seductively at George*)

MRS FLANNEL. Now then, let's have another look at those spots.

(ALBERT *opens his jacket an inch or two*)

That's no good, I want to see how far they extend. (*She turns the bed-clothes down*)

ALBERT (*pulling the clothes back and firmly clasping his jacket about him*) Nay, dammit, I can't go exposing myself.

MRS FLANNEL (*pulling the bedclothes down*) Don't be so modest. You want to get better, don't you? I can't tell what's wrong with you till I see how many you've got. (*She pulls the back of his pyjama jacket over his head*)

ALBERT (*clutching his jacket across his chest*) Help! George! Don't just stand there! Do something.

(MRS FLANNEL *pulls the back of the jacket down over his face.* ALBERT *struggles.*

CLARA *enters up* L, *carrying a suitcase. She dumps the suitcase in the lobby*)

GEORGE. Oh, no!

CLARA. When you've finished undressing my husband, I'd like to have a word with you.

(MRS FLANNEL *releases Albert.* ALBERT *disentangles himself from his pyjama jacket*)

ALBERT. Clara!

CLARA (*moving to the fireplace*) I always seem to be turning up at inappropriate moments, don't I?

MRS FLANNEL. I wonder you have the nerve to turn up at all. For a wife who's supposed to have left home, you seem uncommonly interested in your husband's welfare.

CLARA. And for someone who's supposed to be only a lodger, you seem uncommonly interested in your landlord's underwear.

GEORGE. There's really quite a simple explanation, Mrs Hellewell . . .

CLARA. There always is, but I haven't got time to listen to it. I'll say what I've got to say and then you can get on with the wrestling match.

ALBERT. Don't talk so daft, Clara. We weren't wrestling. Mrs Flannel was only having a look at my back . . .

CLARA. It wouldn't matter to me if she was tattooing it.

GEORGE. It's quite true what he says, Mrs Hellewell.

CLARA. And who are you to speak of truth, George Seegar? From what Elsie tells me, you don't even know the meaning of the word.

ALBERT. Nay, Clara, have some sense . . .

CLARA. I have. Otherwise me and Elsie wouldn't be catching the ten-fifteen train to Blackpool.

ALBERT. To Blackpool? What for?

CLARA. To get away from you two. We're starting work in my brother's fish and chip shop. He wants a couple of assistants for the season.

GEORGE. Elsie can't do that.

CLARA. Why not?

GEORGE. Well—she's got a job here for one thing.

CLARA. She had—up to yesterday.

GEORGE. You mean she's been sacked?

CLARA. No. She's given a week's notice. But she won't need to stay the week because the office staff are on strike, too.

GEORGE. When did they come out?

CLARA. Last night. And if you two hadn't been so busy carrying on, you'd have known all about it.

GEORGE. Good for them! Did you hear that, Albert? This should bring things to a head all right. I reckon the strike's as good as over.

ALBERT (*with feeling*) To hell with the strike.

GEORGE. What?

ALBERT (*fiercely*) I said to hell with the strike. I've had enough of it!

MRS FLANNEL. Now then, don't get excited.

ALBERT (*shouting at her*) I'll do what I like.

CLARA. Come, come, Albert. That's not the way to speak to your lady friend.

ALBERT. She's not me lady friend, she's only me lodger.

MRS FLANNEL (*chiding him*) Albert! After all you said last night.

ALBERT. What the heck are you trying to do? Give her grounds for divorce.

CLARA. I've got them already.

ALBERT. Clara! You're not thinking of divorcing me, are you?

CLARA. After the way you've been carrying on, I don't see how I can avoid it.

ALBERT. Nay, have a heart. If you do that she'll sue me for breach of promise.

CLARA. Then you'd better make an honest woman of her as soon as you get chance, hadn't you?

MRS FLANNEL. You won't regret it, Albert. I'll make you a good wife.

ALBERT. I don't want a good wife. I don't want a wife at all.

CLARA. Shut up. You'll have what you're given. (*To Mrs Flannel*) If you do take him on you'll have to get used to him snoring.

MRS FLANNEL (*moving to Clara*) I don't mind that.

ALBERT. Nay, dammit, Clara . . .

CLARA. I told you to shut up. (*To Mrs Flannel*) And don't give him too much pocket money.

MRS FLANNEL. No fear of that.

CLARA. Otherwise he'll never be out of the pub.

ALBERT. It's a lie.

MRS FLANNEL. I'll watch him. I've had some before.

CLARA. Insist on him having a bath once a week. And make sure he shaves every day. He'll try and get out of it at week-ends if you don't watch him. Oh, and when you get a house, make sure it's not too near the Greyhound Stadium. It's always best to avoid temptation if you can.

MRS FLANNEL. Oh, I don't think we'll bother to move. This place'll do nicely.

CLARA. I'm sure it will. If it's available by then. Which I very much doubt.

MRS FLANNEL. What do you mean?

CLARA. Well, I understand the new tenants are taking it on a long lease.

ALBERT. What new tenants?

CLARA. Didn't I tell you? I've seen the landlord and given him a week's notice.

ALBERT. What the hell for?

CLARA. Well, I shan't be needing it now, shall I? Seeing I'm going to Blackpool.

MRS FLANNEL (*to Clara*) You mean this is your house?

CLARA. It was.

MRS FLANNEL. But I thought Albert was the tenant.

CLARA. Oh, no. My name's always been on the rent book.

MRS FLANNEL (*moving to L of the bed; to Albert*) Is this true?

ALBERT. Of course it's true.

MRS FLANNEL. So you've been leading me on.

(CLARA *sits in the armchair above the fireplace*)

ALBERT (*indignantly*) Leading you on?

MRS FLANNEL. Dangling your prospects before me in the scullery!

ALBERT. I never did.

MRS FLANNEL. Making out you were a man of substance.

ALBERT. Well! I'll go to our house!

MRS FLANNEL. You haven't one to go to!

(*There is a knock on the door up* L)

GEORGE. I'll get it.

(GEORGE *crosses to the door up* L.
TAPEWORTH *enters* L. *He crosses the room hurriedly, his handkerchief pressed to his nose and mouth. He gives Albert a wide berth.*
TAPEWORTH *exits* R.
ROSIE *enters* L, *following* TAPEWORTH)

ROSIE. I gave him the wrong glass.

(GEORGE *moves into the room, holding a telegram*)

CLARA. Who was it?

GEORGE. Telegram. For you, Rosie.

ROSIE (*taking it from him; simpering*) Thanks, Georgie!

CLARA (*in disgust*) Georgie!

ROSIE. Excuse me. (*She opens the telegram and reads it*) Oh, Mum! (*She goes to Mrs Flannel*)

MRS FLANNEL. What is it?

ROSIE. An offer. For a new show. We're in business again.

MRS FLANNEL (*taking the telegram from her*) Let's have a look. (*Reading it*) Well! You and me had better pack our bags, Rosie. Quick. (*Looking round at Albert*) And after what I've heard here this morning, I won't be sorry to shake the dust of this place off my feet

ROSIE. But how are we going to get to Birmingham by half past two?

MRS FLANNEL. Use your head.

ROSIE. A pair of legs and a thumb's more effective! (*She raises her skirt and gives a hitch-hiker's sign*)

(MRS FLANNEL *and* ROSIE *laugh*)

MRS FLANNEL. That's it. You're catching on quick. (*Looking round at the others who are staring at them in amazement*) Come on, we only give free shows at auditions.

(MRS FLANNEL *and* ROSIE *exit* L, *laughing*)

CLARA. Well, now we've got rid of those two we can get the place cleaned up a bit. (*She rises, moves to the lobby, picks up her suitcase, moves to the bed, puts the suitcase on it, opens it and takes an apron*)

(ALBERT *and* GEORGE *look at each other*)

ALBERT. I thought you said you were going to Blackpool.

CLARA (*putting on the apron*) Do I look as if I'm going to Blackpool?

ALBERT. No, but . . .

CLARA. Don't you want me back, Albert Hellewell?

ALBERT. Of course I want you back.

CLARA. That's what I thought. And that's why I came over to help you out of your predicament. It was obvious you weren't going to help yourself so I had to do something about it.

ALBERT. Then all that business about divorce and going away and letting the house . . .

CLARA. Eyewash. For her benefit. I knew what she'd do when she found out that there wasn't going to be a roof over her head. I've met her type before.

ALBERT. Well, if only we'd known it'd have saved us a lot of bother, wouldn't it, George?

GEORGE (*moving to R of the dresser*) By gum it would!

ALBERT. You see we've been trying to get rid of her as well. That's why I went to bed.

CLARA. Really? And how did you expect to get rid of her by going to bed.

GEORGE (*moving to the head of the bed*) He was supposed to be ill.

ALBERT. With bubonic plague.

GEORGE. But it didn't work, because she's been a nurse. When you came in she was trying to look at his spots.

CLARA. What spots?

ALBERT (*opening his pyjamas*) Lipstick.

CLARA. And I thought you were larking about with her just to make me jealous.

ALBERT. Make you jealous? Nay, Clara, I wouldn't try to do a thing like that.

CLARA. Get away. You've been trying it on for the past two days to pay me back for going on strike. But I wasn't impressed. I knew you hadn't the gumption to start anything serious. But she had to go, because I couldn't say the same for her. It was quite obvious she had more than her fair share of gumption. (*She picks up the suitcase, moves to the fireplace and puts it down, L of the armchair above the fireplace*)

ALBERT. Do you know something, Clara? I hate to admit it, but I think you're right.

(*They all laugh.* ALBERT *gets out of bed, moves to the armchair below the window, picks up his dressing-gown and puts it on.*
    TAPEWORTH *enters R, holding his handkerchief over his mouth and nose. He crosses the room to the door L.*
    TAPEWORTH *exits L*)

CLARA. What's up with him?

ALBERT. He thinks I've got bubonic plague.

GEORGE. He was the only one we fooled.

ALBERT. And if he's looked the symptoms up in his B.M.D., I reckon we won't be seeing him around much longer either.

(ELSIE *enters up* L)

ELSIE (*moving to* R *of the armchair above the fireplace; to Clara*) Auntie Dora wants to know if we're still going to stay with her, now that the strike's over.

ALBERT. Over? When?

ELSIE (*coldly*) I was speaking to mum.

ALBERT. Who says the strike's over?

CLARA. Arthur Shackleton.

GEORGE. How does he know?

CLARA. He was at the meeting this morning. He called in at Dora's just after breakfast, on his way home.

ALBERT. Then you knew all the time?

CLARA. You don't think I'd have considered coming back if it had still been on, do you? I've got me principles to consider.

ALBERT. Well, blow me down!

CLARA. You can tell Auntie Dora that we'll be moving out and coming back here this afternoon.

ELSIE. We might be moving out, but as far as I'm concerned there'll be no question of me coming back.

CLARA. What are you talking about?

ELSIE. I've been thinking things over, and I've decided to go away.

CLARA. Go away?

ELSIE. Yes. I can't very well stay in this neighbourhood after all that's happened.

GEORGE. Now look here, Elsie . . .

ELSIE. Don't you speak to me, George Seegar. I never want to see you again.

GEORGE. But the strike's over—finished.

ELSIE. And so are we.

GEORGE. But you only broke off our engagement because of the strike.

ELSIE. It was lucky I did or I'd never have found out the truth about you until it was too late.

GEORGE. I was only paying you back. If you hadn't gone out with Ernest Parsons, I wouldn't have started anything with Rosie.

ELSIE. I don't believe you. It was quite clear last night that you'd been carrying on with her for some time.

GEORGE. I never set eyes on her until yesterday.

ELSIE. Do you expect me to believe that?

GEORGE. It's true, isn't it, Albert?

ALBERT. Aye, of course it's true. I only introduced them a few minutes before you came in.

GEORGE. It was all a put-up job just to make you jealous.

ELSIE. Put-up job, my foot. You were too obviously enjoying yourself.

GEORGE. I wasn't enjoying myself. I was scared stiff.

ALBERT. That's right, Elsie. He told me so himself. She wouldn't leave him alone after you'd gone.

GEORGE. That's why I had to get rid of her.

ELSIE. Get rid of her?

GEORGE. Yes, she's going.

CLARA. And her mother as well.

ALBERT. They're upstairs packing now.

CLARA. I might be a bit dense, George, but I don't see how you can take the credit for shifting them. If it hadn't been for that telegram offering them a job . . .

GEORGE. And who do you imagine sent that telegram?

ALBERT. You mean it was you?

GEORGE. It's a good job they were too excited to notice the postmark.

ELSIE. Oh, George!

(GEORGE *goes to* R *of Elsie*)

ALBERT. So that's what you meant when you said you'd started one line of action . . .

GEORGE. That's right. It's a good job it worked.

CLARA. Oh, I don't know. If it hadn't I reckon I could have shifted them, given another five minutes.

GEORGE (*to Elsie*) Am I forgiven?

ELSIE (*nodding*) Uh huh.

GEORGE. You believe me now?

ELSIE. Of course I do.

(GEORGE *kisses Elsie*)

Do you know something? You were right about Ernest Parsons. He is a drip.

(GEORGE *and* ELSIE *kiss again.* ALBERT *crosses to his jacket which is on the back of the chair* L *of the table, feels in one of the pockets and takes out the engagement ring*)

ALBERT (*crossing above the bed to George*) Here, I think you'd better have this back before I'm tempted to pawn it.

(GEORGE *takes the ring and slips it on Elsie's finger*)

I shan't be so flush next week when the lodgers are gone.

(GEORGE *kisses Elsie again*)

Well, I reckon this calls for a celebration. (*He moves to the dresser and takes out some bottles and glasses which he puts on the table*) Here we are, beer or sherry?

CLARA (*crossing below the bed to the table*) Sherry for me.

ALBERT. How about you two?

(GEORGE *and* ELSIE *do not hear him*)

Come on, break it up. You'll get plenty of time for that later.

GEORGE (*breaking the embrace*) I'll have a beer.

ALBERT. Sherry for you, Elsie?

ELSIE. Please, Dad.

(*There is a burst of general conversation and laughter as* ALBERT *pours out the drinks.* ELSIE *and* GEORGE *move to the dresser.* ALBERT *gives them a glass each.*

MRS FLANNEL and ROSIE enter L, *dressed for departure. The laughter dies away suddenly*)

MRS FLANNEL. Well, well, we are friendly all of a sudden, aren't we? What's going on? Armistice celebrations?

(*There is a silence*)

Or is it somebody's birthday?

ROSIE. From the look on their faces it might even be a funeral party.

ALBERT. I reckon you're not far wrong at that. We're just about to drink to the dear departed.

MRS FLANNEL. Well!

ALBERT. How about one for the road?

MRS FLANNEL. No, thanks. It would choke me.

ALBERT. You might be glad of something warm inside you if you get a lift on an open lorry.

MRS FLANNEL. There's no danger of that. We have our own transport. (*She moves to the lobby*)

ROSIE (*following Mrs Flannel*) And our own chauffeur.

MRS FLANNEL (*she turns and calls*) Benjamin. Come along! We're ready.

TAPEWORTH (*off*) Coming.

(TAPEWORTH *enters* L, *staggering under a load of suitcases, handbags, umbrellas, overcoats, etc.*)

MRS FLANNEL. We'll wait for you at the car.

(ROSIE *and* MRS FLANNEL *exit up* L)

CLARA. Mr Tapeworth, are you going too?

TAPEWORTH. I'm afraid so. One must follow one's bread and butter. You see I've got a new job.

(TAPEWORTH *staggers out up* L. *There is a general burst of laughter*)

ALBERT. Well, come on, lift up your glasses. Here's to the end of the strike. And may we never have another one as long as I live.

(*They all drink*)

GEORGE. Don't forget our engagement.

ELSIE. Re-engagement.

(GEORGE *and* ELSIE *drink*)

CLARA. And the end of lodgers in this house.

ELSIE. Here! Here!

CLARA. And may our menfolk keep out of the clutches of designing females in the future.

ALBERT. Don't worry. You and Elsie are the only women who'll ever set foot in this house again.

CLARA. I should hope so. If ever you entertain any more fancy women I go on strike for good.

ELSIE. Me, too!

ALBERT. No fear of that.

(*Female voices are heard off* L, *calling* "*Albert*")

CLARA. What's that?

ALBERT (*to George*) Yvonne!

GEORGE. Estelle.

ALBERT. Oh blimey, I'd forgotten all about them.

(ALBERT *and* GEORGE *move towards the door* R.

YVONNE *and* ESTELLE *enter* L. *They are young and attractive and dressed in tights*)

YVONNE. Ah, there you are! Is the coast clear?

ALBERT. Eh?

ESTELLE. You know—for us to get a bit of practice in.

YVONNE. You said it would be all right down here when no-one was about.

CLARA (*to Albert*) So!

ELSIE (*to George*) After all you said!

(ELSIE *and* CLARA *advance menacingly*)

GEORGE. There's really quite a simple explanation.

ALBERT *and* GEORGE *back away through the door* R *as—*

the CURTAIN *falls*

FURNITURE AND PROPERTY PLOT

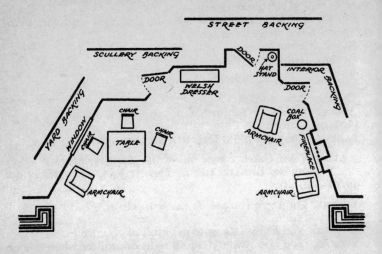

ACT I

Scene 1

On stage: 3 armchairs

3 upright chairs

Dining-table. *On it:* tablecloth, 3 cups, 3 saucers, 6 plates, 6 knives, 6 forks, butter dish, 3 teaspoons, cornflake packet, 3 fruit dishes, table mats, cruet, sugar bowl, milk jug,

Welsh dresser. *On it:* fruit bowl, ornaments, tray, loaf of bread on bread board, bread knife

In racks above: plates, cups, jugs

In cupboard below: cheese on dish, 10 bottles of beer, 6 tumblers, 1 bottle of sherry, 2 sherry glasses, frying-pan, primus stove

Hat-stand. *On it:* Albert's cap, jacket and muffler, Elsie's hat and coat

Hanging from the mantelpiece: Elsie's stockings

Over the mantelpiece: mirror

In the door to the scullery: key

Fire-irons

        Fender
        Fire-screen
        Hearth rug
        Coalbox with removable lid
        Door mat in the lobby. *On it:* 2 letters, morning paper
        Window curtains
        Pictures on walls
        Carpet on floor
        Electric pendant
        Light switch (lobby up L)
Curtains open
Fire lit
Light off

Off stage: Pot of tea and plate of toast (CLARA)
          Suitcase (GEORGE)
          Dirty sheets (CLARA)

Personal: GEORGE: £2 10s. in notes, wallet
         TAPEWORTH: brief-case. *In it:* papers. Umbrella, horn-rimmed
                 spectacles, bowler hat

SCENE 2

Strike: Loaf of bread
      Bread board
      Bread knife
      Beer bottle
      Key
      Newspaper
      Tumbler
      Frying-pan
      Primus stove

Set: *On the dresser:* 2 plates, cruet, butter dish, vase of flowers
     On the hat-stand: Clara's hat and coat
Close the curtains
Light on
Fire lit

Off stage: *In the scullery off* R: Plate of bacon, eggs and chips (CLARA)
                     Teapot (CLARA)
                     Hip bath (ALBERT)
                     Tumbler of water (ALBERT)
                     3 buckets of water (ALBERT)

Off up L: Suitcase (Mrs Flannel)
            Suitcase (Rosie)
Personal: George: cap, newspaper, box of matches
           Elsie: engagement ring
           Tapeworth: brief-case, dressing-gown, sponge bag, attaché-case. *In it:* 4 small bottles containing pills, throat spray, bottle of mouthwash, tumbler, bottle of bath salts, thermometer

ACT II

Strike: Crockery on table
          Hip bath
          Brief-case
          Dressing-gown
          Attaché-case and contents

Set: *On table:* 2 empty beer bottles
                   2 tumblers of beer
                   Crockery and cutlery
        On dresser: tray
        On mantelpiece: safety-pin
Curtains closed
Light on
Fire lit

Off stage: *In the scullery* R: cup of coffee (Mrs Flannel)

Personal: George: cigarettes, lighter, handkerchief
           Albert: buttons, braces, napkin
           Tapeworth: brief-case. *In it:* papers. Umbrella, bowler hat
           Rosie: kimono, brassiere, briefs
           Mrs Flannel: needle and cotton

ACT III

Strike: Tablecloth
          Cup of coffee
          Brief-case
          2 empty beer bottles

Set: Camp bed. *On it:* Albert's pyjamas, bedding

    On back of chair L *of table :* Albert's jacket, engagement ring in pocket
    On armchair R: Albert's dressing-gown
    On mantelpiece : letter O.H.M.S., trinket box. *In it :* box of powder,
        powder-puff, lipstick
Curtains open
Light off
Fire off

Off stage :   *Off up* L: suitcase. *In it :* apron (CLARA)
                suitcases, handbags, umbrella and overcoats (TAPE
                    WORTH)
        Off R: tray. *On it :* 2 tumblers of water (ROSIE)

Personal :   ALBERT: razor, towel, shaving mug, brush and soap
         CLARA: handbag. *In it :* 3 £1 notes
         TAPEWORTH: handkerchief
         GEORGE: telegram

LIGHTING PLOT

Property fittings required: electric pendant c, firegrate (both practical)

Interior. A living-room. The same scene throughout

THE APPARENT SOURCES OF LIGHT are, in daytime, a window R; and at night, an electric pendant c

THE MAIN ACTING AREAS are at the table RC, at the armchair LC, at the dresser up C and C, and down L

ACT I, SCENE 1. Early morning in spring

To open: Effect of early morning sunshine on the window backing R, and
            the street exterior up L
            Light fitting off
            Fire on
            Strips outside doors R and L, on

No cues

ACT I, SCENE 2. Evening

To open: Blue outside window and door up L
            Light fitting on
            Fire on
            Strips outside doors R and L, on

No cues

ACT II. Evening

To open: Lighting as Act I, Scene 2

No cues

ACT III. Morning

To open: Lighting as Act I, Scene 1

No cues

EFFECTS PLOT

ACT I

SCENE 1

Cue 1   ALBERT: "... the place into a blooming dosshouse." (Page 10)
Knock on door up L

SCENE 2

Cue 2   ALBERT: "... your bath should be ready by then."   (Page 25)
Loud banging off L

Cue 3   ALBERT. "What?"   (Page 25)
Loud banging repeated off L

Cue 4   ALBERT: "... I don't think there's 'owt better than Epsom's myself."   (Page 26)
Loud banging repeated off L

Cue 5   ALBERT: "... mind the bucket."   (Page 26)
Loud crash off R

Cue 6   TAPEWORTH: "I'll just nip upstairs and get my nightshirt."   (Page 28)
Knock on door up L

ACT II

Cue 7   GEORGE: "Oh, did you?"   (Page 43)
Laughter off R

Cue 8   GEORGE: "No, I don't suppose you are."   (Page 44)
Scraping noise outside the door up L

Cue 9   ROSIE: "I'll put it on and show you, if you like."   (Page 44)
Door knob of door up L *rattles*

Cue 10   GEORGE: "Do you think he'll make it?"   (Page 54)
Crash off L

ACT III

Cue 11   GEORGE: "... pop into bed quick."   (Page 61)
            Footsteps approaching off L

Cue 12   GEORGE: "... there's no time to argue. Get into bed." *(Page* 64)
            Voices and footsteps off L

Cue 13   MRS FLANNEL: "You haven't one to go to."   (Page 70)
            Knock on door up L

Character costumes and wigs used in the performance of plays contained in French's Acting Editions may be obtained from Charles H. Fox Ltd., 25 Shelton Street, London WC2H 9HX.

Printed and bound in
Great Britain by Butler & Tanner Ltd,
Frome and London